Do I Feel Better Yet?

Do I Feel Better Yet?

Questionable Attempts at Self-Care and Existing in General

Madeleine Trebenski

CHRONICLE PRISM

The following essays were originally published on *McSweeney's Internet Tendency*: "I Got My Bangin' Beach Bod from an Evil Sea Witch and So Can You!," "My Life Has No Meaning, but Have You Tried the New Toaster?," "The Ten Commandments of Workism," "Anything Men Can Do I Can Do Bleeding," "I'm Your Outdoor Dream Girl and Not an Evil Wood Nymph Who Wants to Steal Your Soul."

Library of Congress Cataloging-in-Publication Data available.

ISBN 978-1-7972-1254-8

Manufactured in the United States of America.

MIX
Paper from
responsible sources
FSC™ C005010

Design by Pamela Geismar.
Cover design and interior handwriting by Alex Merto.
Author photograph by Rob Stone.
Typesetting by Happenstance Type-O-Rama. Typeset in Minion and Avenir.

10 9 8 7 6 5 4 3 2 1

Chronicle books and gifts are available at special quantity discounts to corporations, professional associations, literacy programs, and other organizations. For details and discount information, please contact our premiums department at corporatesales@chroniclebooks.com or at 1-800-759-0190.

CHRONICLE PRISM

Chronicle Prism is an imprint of Chronicle Books LLC, 680 Second Street, San Francisco, California 94107

www.chronicleprism.com

For my mum and dad, who have always tried
to make me feel better about everything.

Contents

Have You Tried Buying Things?

Have You Tried Love, Sex, or Some Combination of the Two?

Have You Tried Nature?

Have You Tried Religion or Something That Resembles a Religion?

Have You Tried Relaxing?

Have You Tried Taking Care of Something Other Than Yourself?

Have You Tried Everything?

IF YOU'VE EVER DARED TO EXPRESS A NEGATIVE FEELING about the state of your life—whether it's because of physical discomfort, nagging dissatisfaction, or just general unhappiness—you've probably received various suggestions, both wanted and unwanted, on how to fix it. Maybe you've told your parents you're stressed, and they've replied, "Have you tried working out?" Maybe you've gone looking for answers to your problems on the internet with search terms like "crystals for anxiety?" or "depression in my microbiome?" and gotten answers like, "Have you tried reiki?" or "Have you tried probiotics?" Or maybe you've explained your chronic back pain to your coworkers while lying on the floor next to your desk, and ended up with questions like "Have you tried a standing desk?" or "Have you ever heard of cryotherapy?"

I've found that the more I make it known that I'm some amount of sad, angry, hurting, worried, or stressed, the more well-meaning advice I'm likely to get on how to make it better.

Have you tried:

- Meditation?
- Pilates?
- Getting up at dawn every day?
- Drinking vinegar every morning?

- This $30 adaptogen dust?
- Intermittent fasting?
- Eating only raw foods?
- Setting aside just fifteen minutes a day for you time?
- Setting aside just fifteen minutes a day for you to intermittently drink raw vinegar and eat adaptogenic fasting dust before doing a meditative Pilates session at dawn?

I both love and hate these kinds of suggestions, and I get them frequently. Because, for whatever reason, I seem to be more willing than most people to let everyone around me know when I'm not okay; maybe my brain is a bit broken, or I'm missing some important social filter. For better or worse, I get an above-average amount of helpful suggestions for how to take care of myself, and I've tried a fair number of them at this point. I love the momentary burst of hope they give me. What if this one thing is the answer to it all? But I also kind of hate them because what if a tangible solution isn't always what I'm looking for when I tell people I'm not okay?

After I try most things, I find myself thinking, "Did it work? Am I fixed? Do I feel better?" It can be incredibly hard to tell, especially since I'm not confident that I've ever known what it feels like to be 100 percent okay. The truth is, it can be surprisingly difficult to differentiate between decent advice (exercise provides good endorphins) and utter nonsense (sticking a jade egg up your vagina provides healing energy). It seems safe enough to trust suggestions like sleeping more, eating vegetables, and getting your heart rate up occasionally. But what about the more difficult to pin down promises of things like: fad diets, dream jobs, antiaging face masks, scented candles, fancy underwear sets, gratitude journals, matcha lattes, energy healing, aromatherapy, hypnotherapy, flotation therapy, green juices, acupuncture, urban farming, herbal supplements, astrology, eye creams, nature bathing, obsessive hydration, and cleaning appliances equipped with artificial intelligence? Does any of that stuff make you feel better? And how do you know for sure? How does one measure the effectiveness of a vaginally inserted jade egg?

All the preceding suggestions, whether they're legitimately helpful or not, get lumped under the umbrella of "self-care." Maybe this term was once just a helpful reminder to take care of yourself, but more and more it seems to be used as a catchall— the ultimate solution to every little ache, pain, wrinkle, or insecurity in your life:

Feeling down?

Have you tried self-care?

Feeling burned out by your demanding job?

It's time to practice some self-care.

Suffering from some mysterious stress-related pain that doctors think is psychosomatic?

You just need a little self-care!

The definition of what counts as "self-care" seems infinitely expandable to cover anything and everything you could possibly want to justify. I wouldn't be surprised to see it used as a legal defense someday: "Your Honor, my client had to rob that bank— it was an act of self-care."

The thing is, despite my skepticism of the term and all that comes with it, I've fallen for its promises on numerous occasions. Don't we all attempt to fix complex mental health and lifestyle issues with an essential oil diffuser at least once in our lives? I know I'm not the only one who has thought that drinking homemade kombucha, doing hot yoga, or owning handmade ceramics was going to single-handedly solve all my problems.

Some of my attempts at feeling better have been extremely dumb, some have kind of worked, and some were brief hallucinations that never actually happened. For this book, I've gathered them into a collection of stories, jokes, and occasionally utter nonsense, and organized them according to the following categories: exercise, food, work, buying things, love/sex, nature, religion, relaxation, and taking care of something other than yourself. I can't claim to be an expert on any of these subjects, but I'm going to offer up my thoughts anyway—mostly based on what I've learned from being so incredibly wrong so many times.

It's worth noting here that nothing I write is meant to be taken as serious advice. I'm not a very serious person, and giving advice is for someone who knows what they're doing with their life, not someone who once bought an expensive weighted blanket to help with their anxiety and ended up giving themselves a claustrophobic panic attack instead. Listening to me too closely would be like letting the serotonin deficient lead the potentially serotonin deficient right off the maybe-I-can-find-happiness-somewhere-outside-of-myself cliff.

What I'm hoping is that my mostly failed attempts at self-care will make you laugh, make you feel less alone, and maybe even make you feel better for just a little while. I don't think anyone has all the answers, but I also think it's fun to keep looking for them anyway. Hence, why I'm still asking myself that elusive question I may never have the answer to: Do I feel better yet?

Have You Tried Exercise?

ON PEDALING, RUNNING, BENDING, AND MICRO-PULSING YOUR PROBLEMS INTO SUBMISSION.

Have You Tried Endorphins?

IF YOU'VE EVER BEEN IN A BAD MOOD, OR A VERY PRO-
longed bad mood, or a clinically diagnosed bad mood, there is a
very good chance that some well-meaning person has suggested
to you that exercise might help. "Why don't you go for a run; it
releases endorphins!" This is both very annoying and technically correct. Science has shown that the endorphins your brain
releases during exercise are structurally similar to morphine—
though not similar enough to cause an epidemic of people
addicted to exercise. Endorphins are basically natural painkillers
that reduce stress and produce an almost euphoric feeling of well-
being. Unfortunately, in order to benefit from them, you do have
to haul your body off whatever horizontal surface you're lying
prostrate upon and find the strength to elevate your heart rate.
Panic attacks, sadly, do not count toward this goal.

It's a cruel irony that physical activity is so strongly linked
to mood improvement because vigorous movement is the last
thing I want to do when I'm beset with an unwanted bout of
malaise. If my brain can produce these miracle endorphins, then
why isn't there also a natural trigger that makes me want to join
a CrossFit gym every time I fall into an emotional slump? When
you're overwhelmed by stress, your body knows to make you cry
so it can release that pent-up tension and emotional pain. Why

couldn't the next step (after cathartic sobbing) be an overpowering urge to run sprints and generate endorphins? Instead, here are the solutions my highly evolved human brain offers up:

- *Lying down forever.* That seems like it could really improve the situation.

- *Copious amounts of cheese and sugar.* I'm thinking pizza and cookies—or maybe a pizza that is a cookie.

- *Scrolling through social media for hours.* We could look at some people who are more successful than us, or maybe just some people we knew from high school and college who are buying homes and having babies. We can tell ourselves that they're not as happy as they look, because all social media is inherently performative and people only selectively post the moments from their lives that they want us to see, but we'll still internalize the idea that they're happier than us anyway. It'll be fun!

- Oh! Oh! Oh! Let's watch all eleven seasons of *Frasier* for the third time!

At no point during a spell of abject misery do I ever think, "Wow, I want to run three miles and flip a tractor tire." And it's a shame, because the few times I've found the willpower to put on running shoes and drag my weary bones around the block, it's helped me claw my way out of The Darkness.

It makes me wish that someone would create a gym that specifically caters to sad, stressed, and anxious people. It would be called "Planet Emotional Fitness," and the tagline would be something like "Sweat it all out," or "The only place where it's normal to cry in public, besides the streets of New York." You wouldn't have to work up the motivation to go to this gym because they'd come and get you. The gym itself would offer the following equipment and training programs:

- A bed where you lie under a weighted blanket, and just do reps of lifting the blanket off yourself and getting out of the bed.

- An area where you watch five minutes of television, then get interrupted by a thirty-second commercial. Before the commercial ends you must sprint fifty yards, pick up two heavy bags of snacks—preferably something dense like those one-pound bars of chocolate they sell at Trader Joe's or bulky like a twelve-pack of LaCroix—and sprint back to the TV. You can eat the snacks if you make it in time, but also it's going to happen again in five minutes.

- A treadmill linked to a projection of your Instagram feed that only scrolls if you move forward.

- A yoga class that's just forty-five minutes spent curled up in the fetal position.

- A "praising bag," which is a modified punching bag that speaks words of affirmation every time you hit it. Things like "You are enough," "Plenty of people don't find success before they turn thirty," and "Good job for putting on real pants today."

Once you made use of all the special equipment and programming, your emotional fitness trainer would give you a hug, run you a hot Epsom salt bath, and make you a delicious, nutritionally balanced protein shake—spiked with half a Xanax. After you were fed and fully moisturized, they'd wrap you in a fluffy hotel bathrobe and deposit you back at your home to enjoy the magical benefits of the endorphins now coursing through your veins. If anyone wants to take this idea and make it real, I will be your first customer.

On the opposite end of the spectrum, some people rely on exercise a bit too much for their emotional stability. I'm not saying you can't run ten ultramarathons and be a happy, stable person, but when you start running that far, I start to wonder what you might be running from. However, since our fitness-obsessed culture places a higher value on people who are active, self-motivated, and physically fit (but only if you're also thin because fatphobia), it can feel like there's no such thing as over-doing it. Even writing the word "overexercising" feels a little silly, like saying someone is over-donating to charity or over-saving the whales. But I think there can be too much of a good thing. At the very least, I think it's good to plan for how to manage your stress when your knees eventually give out. And they will give out at some point—that's the number one rule of knees. They're one of the most shoddily made body parts, right after tonsils and the appendix, so you have to be careful if you're depending on them for your happiness.

That said, I do understand how you can get carried away when you find a form of exercise that you truly enjoy. I experienced this feeling myself when I decided to buy a Peloton. You're either rolling your eyes at that or nodding with gleeful under-standing. If it's the second one, you're probably also part of the Peloton cult. I call it a cult because I give them all my money, I can't leave now that they've hooked me, and I worship my favorite instructor, the endlessly entertaining god of stationary biking, Cody Rigsby. It's also the only form of exercise that I've found genuinely enjoyable since playing sports in high school, probably because it's the closest thing I've ever found to a real-life version of Planet Emotional Fitness. There are no weighted blanket reps or Instagram-scrolling treadmills, but it is a lot like having your own personal life coach trapped inside a piece of exercise equipment. Not only does Cody guide me through the necessary physical movements, he also guides my brain away from thoughts like "This hurts," "I can't do this," and "If I die while clipped into this bike, grasping its handlebars for dear life, will firefighters have to cut my rigid body off it with a special saw so my family can give me a proper burial?" I don't just like the bike because it's physically beneficial to spin my feet around in little circles. I like it because it comes with someone who keeps my head from spinning in circles of anxiety and self-doubt while I work out.

As much as I like my bike now, it took me a long time to work myself up to getting one. There were financial considerations first and foremost, but I also kept thinking about what kind of person it would make me. If I bought it, I would have to use it regularly to make it worth the investment. Would regular use turn me into a full-blown exercise addict? Would I start telling people to "try exercise!" in the same way I'd always found so annoying? I had visions of myself becoming a self-righteous fitness influencer, offering people on the street unsolicited advice about interval training and plant-based protein powder. This was, of course, ridiculous. I wasn't going to ride my bike a few times and suddenly undergo a nonsurgical Peloton lobotomy, changing my entire personality.

Despite what some people might have you think, exercising is not a personality trait. It doesn't say anything about you, other than that you sometimes expend energy by flapping your limbs and moving your body about vigorously. I used to think I was lazy or weak because I didn't enjoy it, but it turns out I just needed a big handsome man in tight shorts to yell Britney Spears lyrics at me. It was silly to think that not liking exercise somehow made me a worse person. After all, liking it certainly doesn't make you a more moral one. In fact, you could be extremely fit, full of happy endorphins, and still be a deranged serial murderer—maybe even a strong, strapping one à la Christian Bale in *American Psycho*.

Questionable morality aside, though, if you're going to chase that exercise high, I would first consider two things: 1) It's not the only way to feel better, so it's totally fine if it's not your cup of tea. 2) If you're going to exercise, try to pick an activity you enjoy, be kind to your knees, and don't worry about what anyone else is going to think. Having a Peloton may get me an eye roll from some people, but it's worth every last discount morphine molecule it pumps into my brain and I can't imagine giving it up. Unless, of course, someone decides to open that gym for the chronically anxious and depressed—just let me know.

I Got My Bangin' Beach Bod from an Evil Sea Witch and So Can You!

HOW DID I GET THIS FABULOUS BEACH BODY JUST IN time for swimsuit season? I discovered a powerful fitness secret passed down from ancient European sailors. In other words, I made a bargain with a half-human, half-cephalopod nightmare of the deep. That's right, I got my bangin' summer body from an evil sea witch and so can you!

You might be wondering how a body resembling that of a demigod could come from something so morally repugnant. The answer is simple: black magic. The malice-fueled powers of an authentic sea witch are full of vital antioxidants that cleanse the body of pollutants while simultaneously polluting your very soul. You don't need to fast. You don't need to do a juice cleanse. All you need is a hefty dose of pure evil!

Now, make no mistake, this is not some fad diet. This is a lifestyle change—one that violates the laws of nature. So, to do this properly, you must fully commit to getting a genuine, verified sea witch. Don't try to cut corners by visiting your local swamp or mountain witch. They simply aren't powerful enough, and you'll only regret it when you wake up to find your muscles morphing back into venomous snakes in the middle of the night.

Once you've located a fully certified sea hag, don't be surprised if she tries to lure you onto a bed of sharp rocks. This is the standard greeting, so be polite and play along. You'll want to give her an offering as soon as possible to prevent her from sucking you into a deadly whirlpool. You'll know you have her full attention when you can no longer hear the deafening wails of drowned sailors. I enticed my wicked lady of the ocean with a pound of putrefied fish guts in a basket woven from my own hair, but you can use whatever you have on hand.

Once you've made your profane bargain, she will most likely cast you back to shore on the waves of a great squall. But fear not, your new beach body will be as indestructible as the island of trash plastic gathering strength in the far reaches of the ocean. That is, as long as you never leave the beach. Should you attempt to do so, you will immediately dissolve into sea foam. But everyone knows that all good fitness plans require some sacrifice. At least you won't have to give up gluten or dairy!

This Full-Body Barre Workout Is the Only Thing You Need to Do Today

IF YOU LOVE SCULPTING AND STRENGTHENING YOUR muscles with teeny tiny movements that set your whole body violently aflame while appearing to maintain the exterior grace and robotic poise of a Stepford wife, then Virtue Barre is for you. A small portion of every second of your time is all it takes to lift, tone, and burn yourself into the healthiest shape of your life—and by "healthy shape" we mean a very specific and largely unattainable shape deemed conventionally attractive by Western society.

First things first: If we're going to get you healthy, you need to stop whatever it is you're doing and join a Virtue Barre studio right this instant. Were you planning on getting the grocery shopping done today? It can wait. Performing open heart surgery? Maybe later. Thinking about how you, and women less privileged than you, are systematically oppressed by a patriarchal society that seeks to control women's bodies? If that's what you're thinking about, who's thinking about your thighs?!

Thankfully, you found Virtue Barre just in time. Before you can worry about all that other stuff, you need to worry about your body. Once we've successfully melted away all your undesirable physical attributes, *then* you can find time for other things— like cultivating a hobby or casting off the yoke of oppression.

Unfortunately, since only 2 percent of the population naturally has the ideal healthy body type we strive for here, you have a lot of work to do. You'll be bending your body to our will in no time, as long as you're willing to give us literally all of your time. Cancel all your plans and get ready to gyrate in unison with twenty other women in a room full of mirrors.

Speaking of mirrors, it's absolutely critical to our process that you watch your most unruly body parts get annihilated in our wall-to-wall mirrors, and you can't do that if they're hiding under cheap loungewear. After you've negotiated the small loan you'll need to afford an unlimited Virtue Barre membership, take a minute to make sure you're dressed appropriately for your first class. Did your leggings cost over $100? Did you purchase the requisite workout top with back straps more intricate than an eighteenth-century corset? Oh, and don't forget to grab a few pairs of our branded Virtue Barre grippy socks. They hold you in place when your muscles start to liquefy and shake like the unstable limbs of a baby deer.

Once you're signed up, properly attired, and committed to doing barre every moment of every day, you'll need to learn some important new terms to keep up with your instructor. The most important of these is "thrusting." We know what it sounds like, but get your head out of the gutter. It's just what we call it when you drive your hips up and under in a repetitive pulsing motion, bringing the genitals forward with force and intent. This motion is the foundation of barre and will transform your body, one completely lust-free pelvic jolt at a time.

You may notice your instructor repeatedly shouting encouraging things like "Squeeze your obliques to create a natural corset!" and "Haven't you always wanted a booty shelf?" and "Let's think long, lean thoughts, ladies!" But this focus on bodily aesthetics is purely to benefit you and your health. We guarantee it's not about conforming or trying to look a certain way for others, and it's got nothing to do with appealing to the male gaze. We don't care what men think at all here at Virtue Barre—maybe that's why you'll almost never see men in our classes! Remember, you're working toward a cinched waistline, flat tummy, tight arms, toned thighs, and a shelflike backside *just for you and your health.*

Our philosophy at Virtue Barre is that busy modern women deserve to take some time for themselves and give it all to us; time where they're free to punish their flabby arms and legs until they shake violently with fatigue, free to internalize the message that they should all be long and lean, like sexy cheetah ballerinas. Together, we can tame your gross, undisciplined body and turn it into a thinner, more palatable configuration of parts—one that definitely isn't someone else's idea of feminine perfection being harmfully projected onto you. If you truly care about your own health and wellness, you'll set aside things like personal growth, relationships, and resisting the forces that seek to oppress you, at least for now. That icky, complicated stuff can wait. Because this full-body barre workout is the *only* thing you need to do today.

A Timeline of My Average Three-Mile Run

Day 1

9:00 a.m.   It's so nice out! I should probably go for a run after work.

6:00 p.m.   I've been invited to after-work drinks. Peer bonding is an important aspect of office culture, which I suddenly care about very much. I can always run tomorrow.

Day 2

9:00 a.m.   Oh good, it's still nice out. Perfect for running.

6:00 p.m.   Had a bad day. Can't run because the official bad day coping ritual requires me to eat an entire cheese board alone in a reclined position with zero interruptions.

Day 3

9:00 a.m.   Fuck. It's raining.

Day 4

9:00 a.m. Still raining.

Day 5

9:00 a.m. Okay, today is the day. Running. It's happening.

6:00 p.m. Time to put on running shoes. Can I wear the same Nikes I wore to work? Are they meant for running, or are they strictly fashion shoes? I guess technically all Nikes are both running and fashion shoes. Maybe I'll get a pair of those running sandals. They're better for your feet. Am I ruining my feet with shoes? Will google that later.

6:02 p.m. I googled it. And I bought toe separators.

6:05 p.m. It's too cold for shorts, but I don't own running pants. Do real runners run in specific running pants? Will the other runners know I'm a fraud if they see me running in generic physical activity pants?

6:10 p.m. None of my sports bras fit. This is shocking despite knowing that they're all from a three-pack purchased at Target circa 2007.

6:12 p.m. Maybe the bras are fine. I can still mostly breathe. Maybe if I pass out from oxygen deprivation, a hot firefighter—who also just happened to be out for a run—will have to give me mouth-to-mouth resuscitation. Unless I pass out near some trash, then rats might eat my face.

6:13 p.m. Worth the risk.

6:15 p.m. Just need to pull up my running playlist. Did I make this the same year I bought the sports bras?

7:24 p.m. New, modernized playlist created.

7:26 p.m. Uh-oh, it's almost dark out. If I go, will I make it back before it's fully dark? Men probably don't have to think about this. It must be nice to have a penis. Except I'll bet it bounces around a lot when you run. That must be weird. Who cares about the dark? I should go. For feminism!

7:27 p.m. Wait, isn't that exactly what last night's female victim on *Law & Order: SVU* said right before they found her stuffed under a bush in the park?

7:28 p.m. I'll go tomorrow morning before work. I should be getting up earlier anyway.

Day 6

7:30 a.m. Snooze button.

7:35 a.m. Snooze button.

7:40 a.m. Snooze button.

7:45 a.m. Alarm off.

9:30 a.m. LATE FOR WORK. LATE FOR WORK.

Day 7

11:00 a.m. I have no weekend plans, but I'm not sad. Not sad at all.

11:01 a.m. I'm perfectly fine and happy and alone and—SAD. So very sad.

11:05 a.m.   I should exercise. Something something about endorphins. Something something about releasing "not depression" chemicals into your brain. All right. Running. We're doing it.

11:30 a.m.   Successfully equipped phone by shoving it in the waistband of my pants. Should I be worried that it's held in place by a drawstring, a hope, and a prayer? Maybe I'll get one of those professional phone-holding arm strap doodads if this goes well.

11:31 a.m.   I'll just run three miles. That was considered a warm-up when I played soccer eight—wait, eleven years ago. Should be easy. A warm-up.

11:33 a.m.   This is fine. See? Running is fine.

11:37 a.m.   I am breathing kind of hard though. Can everyone hear how hard I'm breathing?

11:39 a.m.   Maybe I'll walk for a minute. Just until I catch my breath.

11:45 a.m.   Okay, that's enough. Running again. Yes. I'll bet this is almost a mile.

11:50 a.m.   How is this not a mile yet?! Isn't it supposed to take like seven minutes? That's how long the middle school Presidential Physical Fitness Test said it should take. Come to think of it, why was the president testing the fitness of middle schoolers? Seems weird and sadistic in hindsight.

11:56 a.m.   Oh thank god, a sexy song. I shall harness the power of my repressed sex drive to accelerate briefly.

11:57 p.m. I'm doing it! I AM A RUNNER.

12:00 p.m. I've finally hit my stride—I've . . . I'VE GOT A CRAMP.

12:01 p.m. I am a walker.

12:03 p.m. Ow. Ow. Ow.

12:05 p.m. I might need a walker.

12:13 p.m. Maybe all these people in the park will think I've already run ten miles, and this is my cooldown lap. It's not like they know where I've been.

12:15 p.m. I could've run twenty miles for all you people know! I could be an elite athlete. I could—oh good, I've just hit a mile.

12:20 p.m. I need to go home before I pass out.

12:28 p.m. Fuck, was I running downhill the whole way here? I didn't even know there were hills in the city.

12:32 p.m. Oooo donuts. No. Don't stop for donuts. Focus. Focus on your suffering.

12:40 p.m. I kind of can't believe I'm still running.

12:45 p.m. I might actually make it home without stopping.

12:46 p.m. Okay, well, I have to stop at the crosswalk. That's not a choice, that's self-preservation. What was I supposed to do, sprint in front of a bus?

12:55 p.m. Why did I choose this song? This song is obviously not a running song. Okay, now I'm running slower because of it. My legs have turned to lead. I think I might lay down in the street. I should never have left the apartment. Death take me. Cradle me in your icy arms, oh great equalizer. Hold me to your dark bosom and—is that the apartment?

12:56 p.m. Not today, Death!

12:59 p.m. I'm going to lay down on the stoop. Maybe I'll kiss the stoop. No, that's gross.

1:01 p.m. It's over. It's finally over.

1:02 p.m. This is just like that scene from *The Lord of the Rings* after they throw the ring in the volcano and Frodo is lying there talking about how he can't recall the taste of strawberries or the touch of grass. I get it now, Frodo. I'm sorry I made fun of you for all the times you randomly fall down in that movie. You probably had lead legs too.

1:05 p.m. I will now muster the strength to drag my weary carcass into the shower.

1:30 p.m. Wow. I feel great.

1:32 p.m. I wonder why I don't do that more often?

Thanks to Yoga I'm Less Stressed, More Flexible, and Closer Than Ever to Being a Better Person Than You

WELCOME. MY NAME IS ARNICA CELESTIALBODY, AND I'll be your yoga instructor today. When you're ready, please come off your mat and stand with your feet hip-width apart. Then, take a deep breath into your soft, sedentary belly that is not as tight and toned as mine. As you breathe in deeply, stretch your hands toward the sky as if you're desperately reaching for an escape from your tension-riddled body—that's probably why you're here, right? Because your imperfect body is somehow failing you, unlike my perfect body.

Now exhale and let your arms fall to your sides as you slowly realize that you'd have to come to class regularly for this kind of work to have even the smallest effect on your physical or mental health. Even then, you'd probably still never be as bendy and stress-free as me—I do this five times a day!

That's it . . . now let the feelings of inadequacy wash over you as you bring your arms up once more and wonder how I get my hair to shine like a beautiful flowing horse's mane. Is it a side effect of yoga? Could you be a glossy yoga pony one day too? You'll never find out because you only attend class once every three months.

Go ahead and carefully fold yourself in half and bring your hands to the mat. If you're straining to touch your toes, please know that this has never happened to me and I cannot relate. I can fold into almost any position.

Are you thinking about me having sex yet? If not, walk your legs back behind you into downward-facing dog and think about how you nearly threw out your back the last time you tried doggy style. Meanwhile, I can do every position in the *Kama Sutra* with or without a partner—once you reach enlightenment, the universe is your lover.

Drop to your knees and gently come into child's pose. Did I mention I can orgasm without clitoral stimulation?

As you leave child's pose, inhale deeply and come onto all fours. Notice how my form-fitting top with flattering mesh cutouts doesn't hang off me like a sad, dead elephant skin the way your baggy gray T-shirt does. Loose-fitting clothes can't protect your self-esteem here. Odds are the person behind you can see straight up that oversized shirt. So, arch your back up toward the ceiling like a cat, exhale as you come back to a neutral spine, and accept that you're probably going to unintentionally flash the whole room at some point.

Good, now look up toward the ceiling, curving your spine downward and bringing your attention to my mental health. You can probably tell from the light in my eyes that I'm doing way better than you. I certainly don't have to watch old episodes of '80s and '90s television shows every night to mentally transport myself to a time and place where I feel safe enough to fall asleep. I'm actually so consistently relaxed that I'm probably not physically capable of having a panic attack. It's because all my breathing is deep breathing—I do breathwork without even thinking. My nervous system hasn't spiked since the last time they ran out of turmeric at the coffee shop next door. Have you ever tried a golden milk latte?

Now, please bring your forearms to the floor and place your head between your hands. Resist the urge to curl into the fetal position and sob. Then, straighten your legs and walk them into your torso. We're moving into this more complicated pose so that you might release an endorphin or two before you leave today. Endorphins are the key to both my glowing mental state and my extremely high libido—I mentioned that earlier, right? That my libido is very high and I want sex even during the heaviest days of my period? It's because my awesome yoga body produces stress-relieving endorphins with the same vigor that your not-yoga body produces anxiety hives.

This next step is tricky for people like you who have only been moving their computer muscles for the last five years, so let's do it very slowly. Wrap your hands around your head and curl your legs into your chest. Brace yourself for the chance that I will be forced to pointedly correct your posture before you hurt yourself, deepening your feelings of shame and inferiority. When you're ready, lift your legs into the air to complete the headstand. If you're never ready, that's okay too. Just know that your inability to complete the pose is a reflection of your character. If by some miracle you do manage to wobble up into the pose, use this time to let all those bad thoughts you've been having about me drain out of your head and into the floor.

That's right, I know what you've been thinking this whole time. How could I call myself a certified yoga instructor if I wasn't able to sense the impenetrable cloud of bad energy you've been emanating for the last thirty minutes? As you come out of your headstand, lowering your legs back to your chest and placing your feet flat on the floor, please consider that I might be a totally normal person with the same hopes and dreams and struggles as everyone else.

Then, come into a seated position, resting your arms on your knees, and give all the insecurities you've been projecting onto me a rest. I'm just a normal, relatable human being, who happens to have seventeen orgasms per sexual act and ten thousand hours of yoga experience under my stretchy elastic belt. It's not my fault that it makes me perpetually relaxed, impossibly flexible, and undeniably a better person than you.

Namaste!

Have You Tried Food?

ON EATING "CLEAN," HYDRATING OBSESSIVELY, AND
THE THIN LINE BETWEEN HORNINESS AND HUNGER.

Have You Tried a Fad Diet?

THANKS TO A LIFELONG LACK OF FOLLOW-THROUGH, I always *meant* to try more fad diets than I ever actually tried. I bought some green coffee bean supplements (as seen on *Dr. Oz*) and never opened them. I borrowed my mother's South Beach Diet book and then never read it. One summer during college, I purchased two pounds of lemons and a bottle of Grade B maple syrup with the intention of doing the Master Cleanse, the liquid diet where you subsist on a concoction of lemon juice, maple syrup, and cayenne pepper for a minimum of ten excruciating days. I never even made the mixture.

In the case of the Master Cleanse, I was lured in because it promised not only weight loss, but full body detoxification. It wasn't just going to make me thinner; it was going to fix whatever eating pepperoni rolls once a week and drinking banana schnapps out of a CamelBak does to a person. But, for some reason, it just never felt like the right time to stop eating solid food. I guess I'd grown attached to it. Probably due to its essential life-sustaining properties and tendency to create feelings of immense pleasure and well-being. It was almost as if there was no good time to willingly subject myself to prolonged nutritional deprivation.

This mentality also prohibited me from participating in juice cleanses or any diet trend that suggested switching out meals for some dubiously concocted nutrition shake. It wasn't because I was any wiser than my peers at the time. No, I was convinced— just like every other woman in my social circle—that my internal organs needed to be hosed down with kale juice, but I simply lacked the fortitude to give up my morning bagel sandwich. It felt like every time I turned around, someone in my vicinity, either in my real life or on social media, was doing a liquid diet. Facebook was full of before and after photos. Pinterest was full of cleanse recipes and smoothie-based meal plans. It seemed like everyone was purging themselves of the malevolent solid foods of the past and being reborn as salad-eating phoenixes wearing Lululemon yoga pants. It was around this time that I first absorbed an important tenet of toxic diet culture: Food is both thy savior and thy curse.

Most liquid diets and cleanses imply that all solid foods are a blight upon the body. Their whole usefulness is predicated on the idea that the food you've eaten up until now has somehow been unclean and has therefore made your body impure. This, of course, completely ignores the fact that your body has multiple organs whose job it is to filter toxins out of you. What's up, kidneys? Looking at you, liver. Instead, you're told that the only way to fix this internal impurity—caused by eating the wrong foods— is to abstain from food entirely, while washing out your sullied insides with some proprietary health liquid that is, supposedly, made of the right foods. Only this punishing process can fully scrub away the filth of all those Cool Ranch Doritos and Snickers bars you ate before you knew the truth. Only ten days of unadulterated miracle juice can reconsecrate your flesh temple. Don't get me wrong, I know that smoothies and green juices are good for you in some capacity, but total internal purification seems like a lot to expect from a few sticks of cold-pressed celery.

Even fad diets and wellness trends that don't make it their mission to condemn solid food still tend to treat eating like a problem. Because, according to the wellness industry, the right food is medicine, but the wrong food is basically poison. The wrong foods are why you're tired. The wrong foods are why you're depressed. The wrong foods are why you have intestinal parasites—which can only be removed with a $50 patented parasite cleanse! The wrong foods are why you're fat—one of the worst things a person can be, according to our horrifyingly fatphobic culture. However, which foods are "wrong" is entirely dependent upon which popular wellness trend you're subscribing to at the moment.

The trend I finally managed to try for a while was the Paleo diet. It was supposed to revert my body back to a more natural state, making me thinner, happier, healthier, and more focused—the way humans were before the invention of lasagna and hot-fudge-sundae-flavored Pop-Tarts. You know, back when we chased mammoths across the plains and fire was still the newest high-end kitchen appliance at Williams Sonoma. I chose Paleo because it had the most creative reasoning. Its mythology is more or less that human brains evolved faster than human guts, and therefore our bodies aren't equipped to process "wrong" modern foods like wheat and cheesecake. The idea that we're all still cave people internally is nothing if not a good story. It also doesn't hurt that Paleo still allows some wiggle room for things like eating dark chocolate, experimenting with bread substitutes, and drinking red wine—because who's to say that primitive humans couldn't have found a pile of red grapes fermenting in a puddle somewhere?

While trying to be a good prehistoric dinosaur person, I avoided grains and sugar as often as possible. But even with

Paleo's relatively lax standards—compared to something truly diabolical like Keto or Whole30—it was difficult. You can only say no to birthday cake at the office or donuts brought home by your roommates so many times before life begins to seem pointless. My resolve to continue was already wavering when I came across the book that ruined it for me.

I was killing time at JFK airport—browsing one of the bookstores and trying to convince myself I didn't need a Shake Shack milkshake—when I saw it at the center of the "current bestsellers" display. It wasn't called *Why the Patriarchy Wants You to Be Hungry, Cranky, and Constantly Thinking about Food* or *The Life-Changing Magic of Not Hating Your Very Normal Acceptable Body.* It was a new diet book about the hidden dangers of "healthy" foods that cause disease and weight gain.

When I picked this book up, something in my brain snapped. Before I even opened it, I was furious. Now healthy foods are killing me too? It's not enough to worry about gluten and sugar and dairy and carbs? I also have to worry about vegetables?! That was the one food group I never thought I'd have to fear. Because that's what this book was about. It claimed that some fruit- and vegetable-producing plants carry a protein called lectin, which causes inflammation and digestive issues. These plants are part of the deadly nightshade family, a family that includes tomatoes. They could ruin bread for me, they could ruin potatoes, they could even convince me to replace peanut butter—a technically perfect food—with less satisfying almond butter. But never in my wildest dreams had I imagined they'd come for my red peppers and cucumbers, my zucchini and tomatoes. I cannot tell you exactly why tomatoes were the last straw. Maybe it's because they're in almost every comfort food dish my mum makes, or because tomato season has always been the best part of summer.

But besmirching the good name of the tomato crossed a line for me.

Years of pent-up diet culture frustration had suddenly been unleashed and it all came pouring out in the direction of this book. It felt like the culmination of every fad diet claiming to have the final word on healthy eating, every new research study suggesting my pantry might be full of poison, and all the years I'd spent watching my mental list of "wrong" foods get longer and longer. In this moment of irrational rage, I texted one of my friends.

Me: Tomatoes are bad now!

Friend: What?

Me: I found this book at the airport about deadly nightshades, and it says tomatoes are bad.

Friend: Oh yeah, my aunt is on that diet.

Me: It says eggplants are bad too!

Me: Eggplants are supposed to be the lame healthy food you're allowed to eat on a diet, not the cool, dangerous food that's been forbidden! This is wrong. This is a personal attack.

Friend: When does your flight leave again?

As I bitterly stewed on the contents of the book, I asked myself this question: If I combined Atkins, South Beach, Whole30, Paleo, Keto, and this horrible tomato-hating book, and merged them into one super fad diet, what would be left? If all these diets were as absolutely correct in their healthy-eating philosophies as they claimed to be, then surely mixing them together would result in the healthiest diet of all time. But what would survive the greatest pantry purge in history and make it to the ultimate good foods list? Obviously, water would make the cut. Perhaps kale? Celery? A bit of parsley? The purified, alkaline skin of an apple? The essence of a lemon spritz? The first food candidates that came to my mind were eerily familiar. They were the very same ingredients one might find in a typical green juice—the only substance supposedly pure enough to detox a human body polluted by food. My nonsensical rage-fueled diet math had brought me full circle. Why was "no food" always the only "good" food? I put down the book and walked straight to Shake Shack.

I cannot tell you that drinking a chocolate shake out of spite was the rational response to having my brain snap in two over a random diet book at the airport, but it was incredibly satisfying. I unceremoniously gave up on Paleo after that, and I did my best not to get sucked into any more fad diets. I know some diet plans can be helpful for people struggling with food allergies or chronic health issues, but in my case, diets were usually about control. If I could control how I ate, then I could control how I looked and how I felt about myself. Maybe if I ate enough Swiss chard I could even control my own mortality and live forever, like one of those immortal jellyfish at the bottom of the ocean (What do *they* eat and why aren't we putting it on salads yet?). It wasn't a healthy thought process for me.

The thing is, there are so many factors that go into health and wellness besides diet alone that it's absurd to think that there's only one right way to eat. Healthy eating means different things to different people. For example, most of the fad diets I listed tend to keep the definition of "healthy food" extremely narrow and extremely white. They very rarely take into account what foods are practical or affordable for the average household. And most of them are so restrictive that they're completely unsustainable for most people in the long term.

Whatever the wellness industry would have us believe, kale salads and green juice are not medicine, pizza and donuts are not poison, and no amount of leafy greens will grant you eternal life. It's all just a lot more complicated and a lot less extreme than that. But if you're going to try a fad diet, at least pick one that involves solid food and doesn't besmirch the good name of the tomato.

Are You Drinking Enough Water?

ARE YOU FEELING FATIGUED? BLOATED? UNFOCUSED? Do you have acne? Uneven skin tone? Wrinkles around the parts of your face that move? Are you experiencing headaches, trouble sleeping, general malaise, a weird rash on your left arm, bad weather, higher rates of employee turnover, political polarization, more bugs than usual, and the ghost of a revolutionary war soldier haunting your bathroom mirror? Then you're probably not drinking enough water!

Dry mouth? Drink water! Acne? Drink water! An unhealthy buildup of repressed emotions that have turned into chronic, structurally unidentifiable back pain? Drink even more water! It's a well-known fact that the average person is composed of 70 percent water and you personally are not drinking enough of it. In fact, a good person is composed of about 80 percent water and God herself is a sentient H_2O molecule. I'm not saying you're a bad person if you don't drink the correct amount of water a day for a human adult, but science and God might be saying it.

If you're pretty sure that you're already drinking enough water, just know that you're probably not. Because if you were drinking the recommended eight glasses of water a day, none of which are coffee, you would have glowing skin, impeccable digestion, smaller feet, the answer to lasting world peace, and a popular vlog detailing how water is responsible for all of it. If you truly understood the power of hydration, you would worship it. In fact, you would be so overcome by a deep and overwhelming sense of inner wellness that you wouldn't be able to resist telling everyone within a hundred-mile radius your new fundamental truth: Water is the key to life itself. You might even die without it!

This miraculous realization might lead you to ask deep philosophical questions like, "If water is the key to life itself, then why hasn't it evolved to taste like Cherry Coke Zero yet?" and "Does it refuse to taste like Cherry Coke Zero because it doesn't actually want us to drink it?" Furthermore, why doesn't Cherry Coke Zero count as water when it is also a liquid and also has zero calories? If these cerebral musings seem nonsensical to you right now, don't worry, things will become clearer once you're hydrated.

Thinking you're already hydrated is a very common mistake among the chronically dry and unenlightened. You're so busy trying to earn a living wage and find a therapist who takes your health insurance that you've never had time to notice that the ultimate answer to every one of life's problems is coming out of faucets all around you. Not that you should drink water from faucets—that stuff is poison! Everyone knows you should only drink VOSS water that's passed backwards eight times through a reverse osmosis filtration system and then at least once through Gwyneth Paltrow.

Fortunately for the shriveled, dehydrated husk you're currently inhabiting, it's easy to benefit from the life-changing effects of water almost immediately. All you have to do is drink as frequently as you would during a work happy hour riddled with awkward silences. Drink like a large fish that just spent fifteen minutes gasping for breath so some guy named Aidan could get a photo for his dating app profile. Drink more than all the almond trees in California combined. Drink as if you alone can stop the rising sea levels of global warming by holding the mass of the melting polar ice caps within your body, and don't stop until all of your bodily fluids run as clear as a mountain spring. Don't stop until you take so many bathroom breaks that your friends start to worry about your well-being and your boss threatens to dock your pay. Don't stop until your very DNA begins to resemble that of a large aquatic mammal!

Once you've done this you will be very close to the ultimate goal of complete hydration. If you don't immediately feel like you could run the NYC marathon in record time, peel an avocado without touching it, and launch your own hemp-infused skincare line for moms, it's probably because the water you imbibed was impure. If you don't have Gwyneth Paltrow on hand to pass your water through, any wellness influencer will do. Otherwise, it could be sullied by things like fluoride, chlorine, and the disincarnate souls of an alien race trying to contaminate your body with their negative energy. If that happens, it will take twice as long to flush out the toxins and the disembodied immortal spirits, and you'll have to start hydrating all over again. No one wants that.

Now, the biggest issue for most people is that they just forget to drink. So, to keep hydration top of mind, try lugging around a five-gallon drum of water marked with twelve evenly spaced segments representing the hours in your day. You can even add encouraging phrases to each of your hourly goals to motivate yourself. It should look something like this:

8 a.m.   Rise and chug!

9 a.m.   Keep chugging!

10 a.m.   You should be able to feel it sloshing in your belly now.

11 a.m.   Don't you want perfect skin?

12 p.m.	Your friends have probably had twice as much water as you by now.
1 p.m.	At this point you should have your own internal tidal chart.
2 p.m.	Keep up!
3 p.m.	No excuses.
4 p.m.	Don't disappoint your body like you disappoint your father.
5 p.m.	Quitting is for people with dry skin.
6 p.m.	MORE!
7 p.m.	Stop crying.
8 p.m.	Tear replacement does not count toward the daily quota.

Remember: It will all be worth it. Because once you're properly hydrated there will be nothing that can stand in your way—no ailment that can pierce your protective watery membrane. You shall ascend to a state of liquid perfection and your earthly identity will fall away. You will forget the petty concerns of the past and take on a holy quest to drink every drop of moisture in the known universe, so that you might one day achieve a biological status known only by a select group of staggeringly popular social media influencers. Then, in time, your own disciples will flock to you, and they will kneel before your glowing translucent feet to say things like, "What products do you use?" and "OMG, I wish I had your skin." And you will smile upon them smugly and say, "Are you drinking enough water?"

A Quick and Easy Recipe for Incredibly Haunted Bone Broth

BONE BROTH IS A DETOXING AND DEEPLY NOURISHING food that various cultures around the world have been making for thousands of years. Now, modern cooks are rediscovering its benefits, and it might just be the perfect solution to that nagging, unfounded suspicion you have that your body is full of unidentified malevolent toxins (probably from all the conventionally grown avocados you've eaten). Fortunately, the bone broth we're going to make today is not only incredibly cursed, but also affordable and easy to make at home. All you need is a bunch of bones, a large pot, and the cauldron-stirring stamina of a long-haired, sixteenth-century kitchen witch. We'll have you cleansing those malefic toxins from your mortal coil before you can so much as utter the words, "Isn't that what my liver is for?"

How to Make the Bone Broth

1. *Get some delicious spooky bones.* You can collect your bones from anywhere, but your local butcher, farmer's market, or unmarked burial ground are great places to start. I usually order mine from a centuries-old occult group living deep in the forests of western Germany. They offer a variety of

leftover skeletal remains from their most profane rituals and sacrifices for a very reasonable price (so it's both cheap and sustainable!).

2. *Put your assorted skeleton bits in a pot.* I personally use an iron cauldron forged in the dark fires of an ancient volcano by an evil enchantress seeking to reanimate the dead, but an eighteen-quart stockpot will also work. Fill it four-fifths of the way with remains and add enough cold water to cover them. (TIP: If you have access to holy water, cover the bones with that instead. It's not necessary, but it will rile up the angry spirits, reducing the amount of time needed to boil them out of their earthly prisons and release their complex flavor.)

3. *Bring the mixture to a screaming boil.* Once it begins to writhe and roil, as if the water itself is in unspeakable agony, turn the heat down to a simmer for an hour or two. At this point the pot should cease its violent shrieking and settle into long steady wails of wretched misery. Periodically skim off any toads, snakes, bats, or other familiars of our Dark Lord Beelzebub that may rise to the top.

4. *Chop and mock.* Add organic chopped vegetables like celery, carrots, tomatoes, or onions, but only choose three so as to make a proper mockery of the holy trinity. This is also a good time to add aromatics like peppercorns or chant an unholy incantation in an accursed tongue over the mixture for a bit of zest.

5. *Let simmer angrily for eight to twelve hours.* Check the mixture occasionally to ensure that the accursed bones are not emerging from their confinement to seek vengeance on

those who would wield the dark powers of their deathly essence.

6. *Strain the broth through a piece of cheesecloth or a holy shroud.* Ignore the swarms of bees, crows, and howling black dogs drawn to the call of the broth. They will quiet once it begins to cool.

7. *Season with salt and prayer.* You must call upon the boiled bone spirits to banish the mysterious toxins from your body with their power. As with all exorcism rituals, you must provide the true names of the entities possessing you. Once you've named the suspected toxins, those destructive agents of hypothetical disease that have been plaguing you, they shall be cast out. (I'm sure a quick internet search will reveal which toxins you have—maybe, like, mercury or something? Is cellulite a toxin? You'll figure it out.)

8. *Transfer the broth to a ritualized storage container.* This helps to seal in the freshness and the malignant rage of the bone spirits trapped within (I use a Jewish dybbuk box, but a set of blessed Tupperware will also work). Refrigerate the broth overnight, and don't worry if you or members of your household suffer from horrific dreams involving reanimated corpses and boiling vats of blood. They should stop once you've consumed all the broth.

9. *Skim any threatening messages written in solidified fat off the top.* Then, store the broth for up to five days in the fridge or up to six months in the freezer. Any longer than six months may result in a ravenous otherworldly portal opening beneath the foundations of your home and sucking your entire neighborhood into a spectral plane.

Common Mistakes

1. *Not skimming the fat and familiars from your broth frequently enough.* Skimming removes impurities, which can transfigure into agents of the devil in the blink of an eye. The last thing you want is a bunch of rats doing Satan's bidding in the middle of your soup.

2. *Skimping on your bone-boiling time.* You must boil the bones into submission to harvest the fruits of their wickedness. Bones that have been boiled for at least eighteen to twenty-four hours will be easiest to bend to your will.

3. *Using the bones of evildoers to enrich the power of your broth.* It is a common assumption that adding the bones of the corrupt, immoral, or blackhearted will strengthen the power of your broth. Unfortunately, adding the bones of someone like a dark necromancer or Jeffrey Bezos will only give the broth an unappealing cloudy look. Or worse, it will destabilize the mixture entirely, causing it to erupt in green flames at the mere mention of workers' rights.

Now You've Got Haunted Bone Broth. How Do You Eat It?

These protein-rich broths make a great foundation for soups, stews, sauces, and gateways between the worlds of the living and the dead. They can also be had on their own, sipped from an earthenware mug to enhance the feeling that you're a quaint, old-timey farm laborer with an illegal witchcraft side hustle, and not an urban office worker desperately searching for some spiritual or emotional connection to the natural world.

Possible Health Benefits/Side Effects

Glowing skin. In both the metaphorical "glow of health" sense and the literal "skin made of glowing blue ectoplasm" sense.

A boost to your immune system. All living things will wither and shrink from your presence for up to twelve hours after consumption, including viruses and bacteria.

Total detox. The indeterminate toxins you were once vaguely worried about will be forced to evacuate as your body becomes a temporary host to the simmering essence of death itself—an unquestionable improvement!

Wellness Supplement or Parasitic Space Monster from the *Alien* Franchise?

1. *Lingua foeda acheronsis* is _____.
    a. A probiotic supplement that regulates your vaginal pH.
    OR
    b. Latin for "foul tongue from Acheron."

2. Adaptogens are _____.
    a. A species of extraterrestrial endoparasitoid that adapts to its environment by subsuming parts of its genetic material.
    OR
    b. A wide range of weird, dusty plant materials you can add to your $15 cold-pressed celery juice to make it a $20 cold-pressed celery juice.

3. Cordyceps are _____.
    a. A genus of parasitic fungi that grows mostly on the larvae of insects. Some say it increases exercise performance and fights aging, while others say, "Wait—it grows on insect larvae?"
    OR

b. A genus of parasitic aliens that grow mostly in the chest cavities of human beings. Some say they can increase appetite and cause sore throat, exhaustion, shortness of breath, and hemorrhaging. Others say, "AH! AHHHH! IT'S BURSTING OUT OF MY CHEST! AAaaAaAaaaAAAHHhhgg!!!"

4. Xenomorph is _____.
   a. A term used by some military officials to reference generic extraterrestrial life.
   OR
   b. A zero-calorie sugar substitute that may or may not make you poop immediately after consuming it.

5. A Quinton shot is _____.
   a. The signature attack of the alien species *Internecivus raptus*, in which it shoots forth its powerful inner jaw to pierce its victim's skull.
   OR
   b. A shot of 100 percent raw marine plasma harvested from a plankton vortex off the coast of Spain, which is either great for your nervous system or great if you enjoy drinking wildly expensive filtered sea scum for lunch. Possibly both.

6. Yautja is _____.
   a. The proper name for a species of spacefaring humanoid extra-terrestrials, more commonly known as "Predators," who use their advanced technology to hunt other life-forms for sport.
   OR
   b. Yet another Ayurvedic herb co-opted by white people with little to no understanding of its original context within either modern or ancient Eastern medicine.

7. Chaga is _____.

a. The name for a distinct biological variant of the Predator species most easily identified by a small red gland beneath their clavicle that secretes a hormone capable of throwing them into a homicidal rage.

OR

b. A powdered super mushroom that will balance your energy and make whatever baked good or beverage you're adding it to taste just a little bit weird, no matter how much sweetener you add. All for a mere $37 per ounce!

SHORT ANSWER: +2 bonus points

Which is more frightening? Fictional facehugger aliens that implant parasitic embryos in your body by latching onto your mouth with a grip strong enough to tear flesh, or the fact that dietary supplements are largely unregulated, sold without any requirement for upfront evidence of effectiveness, and have occasionally been found to contain substances like lead, mercury, and other potentially harmful heavy metals?

Answer Key

Multiple Choice: 1. b 2. b 3. a 4. a 5. b 6. a 7. b
Bonus Question: Definitely the facehuggers.

You're Probably Tired Because You Eat Grain, Not Because Your Earthly Consciousness Resides in a Naturally Decaying Flesh Suit That Inevitably Fails as You Age

YOU'VE PROBABLY BEEN TOLD YOUR WHOLE LIFE THAT it's completely normal to have the occasional off day. Everyone has moments where they're just not that focused, where they feel a little foggy, right? Licensed health professionals will tell you it's normal to feel tired sometimes due to the everyday stress of our busy modern lives; that what you need is a bit of rest, a balanced diet, and some stress management techniques. And they would be lying! Because there's a secret that doctors, health officials, and the producers of good-tasting food don't want you to know: Every grain you've ever eaten is a murderous, poisonous killing machine that's slowly destroying your body.

Did you think that overconsumption of alcohol, sugary processed foods, and tobacco products were the biggest dietary threats to your health? These trifling transgressions are nothing compared to the true evil that's been lurking in your diet all along. There is a silent killer in your granola, your bread, your pasta, and your cookies. It's everywhere, and it wants you dead— or at least partially incapacitated by a difficult to diagnose and even harder to treat chronic illness that leaves you susceptible to the seductive claims of charlatans and snake oil salesmen.

Don't believe it? Think about the last time you ate a piece of toast. Did you feel tired later that morning, afternoon, or night? You probably thought your fatigue was due to the normal energy cycles of the human body, but it was almost certainly the toxic machinations of that grain-ridden piece of toast. People don't realize that the human body was never meant to experience weariness, soreness, sadness, decreased libido, bloating, hangnails, chapped lips, stubbed toes, forgetting where you put your keys, or mild discomfort of any kind. We've been told these maladies are just part of living as physical beings, but the truth is that grain is a harbinger of inflammation that's been ravaging our bodies for thousands of years—since our first misguided ancestors planted a field of wheat and doomed us to a ruinous world of bagels and pretzels and Red Lobster Cheddar Bay Biscuits.

Doctors will tell you that grain is only an issue for individuals with celiac disease or gluten sensitivity, but that's because they've been bought off by Big Grain. Why else do you think only nine out of ten doctors on the Cheerios box agree that whole grains are good for heart health? The tenth doctor knows the truth! The other nine are part of the global conspiracy to keep people buying and eating grains, and they have been highly successful. These days you can hardly swing a stick in a grocery store without hitting a loaf of bread or a bag of flour. And you probably get really tired and mentally cloudy from swinging that stick because your whole body is so inflamed by grains.

Fortunately, there's some good news. You don't have to suffer at the hands of these infernal cereal crops anymore. With the Grain-Free Food-Free Live Forever Diet, you can start to wean yourself off grain and watch your health rapidly improve. All you need to do is cut out most foods, but especially the foods you love. Begin by abruptly removing all grains, sugars, and happiness from your diet. Try some of our most popular recipes, like Authentic Mesolithic-Era Leaves and Twigs Salad, Pasta-Free Spaghetti (it's just the sauce!), and a crowd favorite, Six Pounds of Raw Ground Beef Mixed in a Bowl. After a few weeks of eating cleaner, you're guaranteed to start feeling better, thinking more clearly, and sharpening your canine teeth to help with the increased protein consumption. You might also feel positively ravenous, but that's just a result of your newly heightened senses, which were formerly dulled by grain.

This stage of your detoxification is the perfect time to head to grainfreefoodfreeliveforever.com for some of our proprietary supplements, which we forgot to mention are absolutely necessary for completing your diet effectively. Here are the essentials:

1. **Brain Drain.** This product is on the cutting edge of neurotechnology and can be found exclusively on our site. Let the special formula of omega3000 fatty acids—that's 2,997 more omegas than you can find anywhere else—wash your brain of toxins that have been building up for years. It can take up to six months to see noticeable results, but it'll be the best $395.99 you've ever spent cleaning your brain.

2. **Not-Proven-Not-to-Work Probiotics.** This proprietary blend of helpful gut bacteria may or may not inconclusively improve your digestion and overall health. We haven't yet determined what the chances are that it truly does anything, but we do know there's a 100 percent chance you'll spend upwards of $80 for just one jar of sixty capsules. Don't forget to take two twice a day!

3. **Lizard Oil.** You'd be hard-pressed to find a more miraculous remedy than our lizard oil. Made by boiling the skins of a rare desert reptile underneath a full moon, this powerful detoxifier and metabolizer cures the body of everything from unidentified chronic illnesses to feeling kind of "meh" today. You'll know it's working when it starts to bubble gently on your skin and emits a soft hissing noise—that's the sound of the lizards cleansing your cells. Rub your whole body down from head to toe every morning to repair years' worth of grain-inflicted damage on contact. As long as you apply it every day, your cells will continue to regenerate perpetually, making you effectively immortal. Can you believe the low price of everlasting life is just $29.99 an ounce and hunting a small reptile species to the brink of extinction? Side effects may include: itching, burning, dry skin, and smelling like a lizard for the rest of your eternal life.

Now, you may find the Grain-Free Food-Free Live Forever lifestyle hard to stick with at times but rest assured, you were built for it. Humans have specifically evolved to thrive on this diet and the additional man-made, mass-produced supplements it requires. If it's not working for you, it's probably because unnatural grain products, the menu at every single restaurant you like, and years of exposure to FDA-approved forms of sustenance have ravaged your body over time. In this case, we recommend doubling your doses of our supplements. We promise it'll be worth it in the end. Though, technically, there won't *be* an end if you fully commit to this new lifestyle and live the way nature intended—grain-free, food-free, and forever.

Are You Hungry or
Are You Just Horny?

SOMETIMES IT CAN BE DIFFICULT TO DIFFERENTIATE between a late-night craving for pepperoni pizza and the desire to have an orgasm. Is it your appetite for melted cheese? Or is it your appetite for human intimacy? The two feelings can be so incredibly similar that it can take some rather nuanced internal cross-examination to figure out the true object of your desire. To identify the source of your late-night longings, try asking yourself the following questions:

If you order yourself a pizza right now, in an hour or two, will you still find yourself thinking about the way Mr. Darcy clenches and unclenches his hand in the 2005 movie adaptation of *Pride and Prejudice*?

I'm going to ask you to picture a peach in your mind. Did you just imagine a peach? Or Timothée Chalamet and that peach from *Call Me by Your Name*?

If you were to eat a whole sleeve of Oreos, would you be satisfied, or would you still want to look up old *So You Think You Can Dance* couples' routines on YouTube?

What do you really want: a hot fudge sundae, the hot priest from season two of *Fleabag*, or the even hotter inner workings of Phoebe Waller-Bridge's mind?

If I placed Michael B. Jordan on the right side of the room and a cheeseburger on the left side of the room, how quickly would you run to the right?

When I say the word "milkshake," is your first thought of the delicious frozen treat, or the clearly not at all teenage cast of *Riverdale*?

If you're experiencing a strange craving, and you can't pinpoint exactly what it is, ask yourself: Is it salty? Is it sweet? Or is it the poignant, unknowable beauty of Cate Blanchett in *Carol*?

Which one is more enticing: the warmth of spicy tingly beef or the warmth of human contact?

If you chose to eat the whole sleeve of Oreos from earlier, are you biting into them like normal cookies, or are you doing that thing where you twist off the top and slowly lick the filling? If it's the filling thing, you probably weren't hungry.

Are you truly experiencing a craving for hot, sticky cinnamon rolls, or has Tom Hiddleston's portrayal of Loki just made you crave a toxic bad boy with a warm gooey center?

While watching Seo Dan and Gu Seung-jun eat noodles in the Netflix Korean drama *Crash Landing on You*, are you thinking about the noodles? Or what "eating noodles" is supposed to be code for in the world of K-dramas?

Take a moment to think about Jason Momoa holding a cute baby or a small dog. What sound just came from your abdomen? The sound of your stomach growling, or the sound of your reproductive organs exploding?

When I say the words "dark chocolate," do you think, "mmm, dark chocolate" or "dark chocolate → dark side → Kylo Ren → I wish Adam Driver would yell at me → how are his hands the size of dinner plates?"

Could you, right now, eat a banana without thinking about human genitalia? Trick question, no one can.

Finally, the most important question you must ask when trying to decipher whether you are hungry or horny is: Are you just both? Because, honestly, there is nothing but lack of imagination stopping you from having both an orgasm and a snack, possibly at the same time. Sure, being able to correctly identify whether you're experiencing hunger or horniness is a good exercise in self-awareness, but it's not an emotional mandate. As long as you end up fully satisfied, without violating any federal laws, it hardly matters whether it's a pint of ice cream or a person that gets you there.

Have You Tried Working?

ON JOBS I'VE HAD AND JOBS I ONLY WISH I HAD.

Have You Tried Your Dream Job?

"PLEASE DON'T DIE FOR BURGER KING."

Those five words are probably the best career advice I've ever received—besides "Don't sleep with your coworkers." They came from a professor at my grad school who, at the time, seemed to have a particularly bleak outlook on our class's future job prospects. Now, looking back, I see that he was just being realistic.

The advice was part of a story he told about a former student who went to work for a large advertising agency in New York City. They were young, hardworking, passionate about the industry, and they never said "no"—everything a manager could want in an underpaid entry-level employee. They lost themselves in their work each day and stayed late most nights. They were dedicated and tireless and determined to make the best ads their client, Burger King, had ever seen. Until, one night, while working late at the office yet again, they collapsed.

Upon being rushed to the emergency room, they were told that they'd experienced a small stress-induced heart attack—which is really not the way one expects Burger King to give you a heart attack.

After telling his cautionary tale, my professor looked out at the class and explained that we would face this same pressure to work ourselves to the point of exhaustion (I don't think "burnout" was a term then). So, if we didn't want to find ourselves suffering a minor cardiac event for the glory of advertising, we'd have to learn to set boundaries. Because no matter what our employers might say, making internet banner ads to sell french-fry-shaped chicken nuggets for a multinational burger chain was not worth our health and well-being. "Please, don't die for Burger King," he said with a sad look on his face that suggested he already knew that not all of us would heed his warning.

At my first agency job out of school, I witnessed exactly how someone might be driven to the brink of heart palpitations in the name of mass-produced meat patties. This junior-level copywriting position was supposed to be a dream job for someone just starting out in advertising. The office had a trendy minimalist open floor plan, and the job had all the bells and whistles that tech companies, start-ups, and "creative class" industries tend to dangle in front of potential employees. Unfortunately, most of those perks came with a sinister twist. For example:

- A free dinner was served every night at 8 p.m. in the large communal kitchen on the main floor. This sounds like a great perk when you're making an entry-level salary and trying to live in New York City, until you realize that it means enough people are at the office past 8 p.m. every single night to make it worth catering a large group meal.

- If you stayed at the office past 8 p.m. on any given night, you could expense a cab home, which seems nice until you find yourself working until 7 p.m. and then putting in an extra hour just to access dinner and a cab ride.

- There was beer on tap in the main floor kitchen, so you didn't even have to leave the office for happy hour. This perk was promoted to visitors and potential employees as evidence of the office's cool, laid-back vibe, but it lost some of its charm when they started locking the tap outside of official agency happy hours. These usually happened on Fridays, and it wasn't uncommon for people to go down to the kitchen at 5 p.m., have a glass of flat beer, and then go right back to work—fun!

- The bathrooms were stocked with all manner of hygiene and grooming products: mouthwash, hairspray, dental floss, face wipes, spray-on deodorant, hair ties, and bobby pins. Because when you live at the office, you need it to have all the comforts of home.

The general office vibe felt like an episode of *ER* if you replaced the doctors with brand managers and the life-threatening emergencies with six-second social posts and vertically integrated brand strategies. People were constantly running around, clutching their cold brew coffees and bowls of free cereal, as if they were on their way to perform brain surgery. You'd never know that the constant high-stakes drama was in service of selling acne cream and cheese-filled sausages.

Every few weeks, all five hundred employees would be summoned to sit on the grand staircase in the center of the office, which functioned like bleachers at a pep rally. This is where upper management would play video reels of the agency's latest work on the big screen and give rousing speeches about creative greatness. We weren't just making advertisements; we were creating culture. We were lucky to be here and we should be grateful to spend the majority of our waking hours in the company of so much talent—and so much free cereal. We weren't just working at any advertising agency; we were working for the best advertising agency in the world (as voted upon by other people who worked in advertising).

Since ads are considered by most people to be either annoying, dishonest, or a plague upon this Earth, it always struck me as a bit funny to celebrate being number one at making them. It was like saying you were the best at a very specific kind of bullying. The best at bursting into people's homes—unwelcome and uninvited—and attempting to convince them to buy a new brand of toilet paper. In the very best-case scenario, if you said something funny or compelling enough, they might forgive the fact that you were interrupting fifteen seconds of their lives in an attempt to manipulate them, but that still didn't mean they wanted you there. Knowing this made it feel particularly ridiculous when people expected me to pour blood, sweat, and fourteen hours a day into making an "award-winning" toilet paper commercial. I had no problem doing the work that I was paid to do, but why was this worth working the weekend or answering emails at 11 p.m.? Why was every client deadline an emergency? How could there even be such a thing as an advertising emergency?

It's hard to reconcile this absurd reality with the modern idea that we're all supposed to find meaning in our work. According to standard millennial dogma, your dream job is supposed to give you purpose in life. For many people, work itself has become the new religion—a secular path to self-actualization. Part of me bought into this idea while I was still in school—maybe we could change the world with ads about toilet paper if we really tried! But I quickly became disillusioned within my first three months of working, right around the time I worked on what will forever be known as "the infamous squares campaign."

When my partner and I first started—we worked together on all our projects as an art director and copywriter team—we were asked to work on a campaign for a financial client, which would encourage people to save just 1 percent more of their money. For days, I did as I was told by my creative superiors, writing insufferable lines about how $5 lattes could ruin your long-term finances, all while clutching my own $5 latte—its warm caffeinated embrace being the only reason I'd gotten out of bed that morning.

Then, at five o' clock on the day before The Big Meeting, my partner and I were told that the campaign hadn't been approved by our executive creative director. He was an average forty-something-year-old white guy with a hero complex and a tendency to micromanage, and he would be helping us fix it. He was our boss's boss, so we couldn't object to this. In fact, we should be grateful that such a high-level person was willing to swoop in and save the whole campaign from mediocrity at the last minute.

After five hours of tweaking billboard comps, listening to his ramblings about the need for a "groundbreaking way to show people what 1 percent more could do," and dinner in the communal kitchen, inspiration finally struck. The advertising gods spoke to him and said, "Let there be a visual representation of 1 percent in the form of a square." It had all suddenly fallen into place for him. He could see the presentation deck forming before his eyes, and he could finally start delegating our tasks to us. We would make a print ad featuring one tiny square on a solid background, and this square would take up 1 percent of the print ad it occupied. Next to it, there would be a line reading, "This is what *just* 1 percent more looks like." Or maybe, "This is what 1 percent more looks like." He couldn't decide.

Fueled by the desperate hope that we might get home before midnight, we showed feverish enthusiasm for the square idea. It wasn't just clever; it was truly visionary! In a frenzy, we created a whole campaign based on the square: billboards with the square, social posts about the square, an interactive brand activation in

Times Square, featuring the square. We coasted through on pure adrenaline until he gave his final stamp of approval and, at last, released us.

The following day went by in a flurry of demands for larger logos on banner ads and fewer words in Facebook posts before we realized that we hadn't heard anything about the squares presentation. No matter how inane the idea had been, we needed to know that our time, our suffering (our indigestion from last night's catered Outback Steakhouse dinner) had been worth it. When we tracked down the project manager, she gave us an exasperated sigh.

"Oh that? You won't believe what happened with that." She avoided meeting our eyes as she hurriedly explained. Apparently, on the very first slide of the presentation, Karen (the head client) had turned to Stacy (our lead account person) in what appeared to be absolute outrage. Karen had then audibly whispered, "Stacy, you *KNOW* how I feel about squares."

We stood there, baffled, until my partner spoke up. "How does she feel about squares?" The project manager shook her head and said, "Not good. She does not feel good about squares." My partner quietly murmured, "But the whole presentation was squares."

"There were squares on every page," I piped in. The project manager gave us a look of pity as she explained that the presentation had come to a screeching halt around slide three. They'd scrapped the whole thing and decided to do a brainstorming session with the client instead. "Wait, why would Stacy know how Karen felt about squares? Who just hates squares?!" I was asking questions to which there were no answers.

We never got an explanation for Karen's feelings about squares, but it didn't really matter. What mattered was that we'd just worked ourselves to the bone over something that had been rendered instantly meaningless by someone's arbitrary dislike of four-sided polygons. It became achingly clear that this job could not be the thing that gave us purpose. It would be like committing ourselves to a foul-tempered mercurial god who demanded everything, including nights and weekends, while promising us nothing but the empty consolation prize of "advertising fame" in return. Despite all of upper management's promises of creative fulfillment and claims of greatness, this was still just a job. It was barely worth the money it paid us, and giving it more of ourselves than was strictly necessary was pointless self-sacrifice in the name of a thankless work-based religion.

After this experience, and the many more traumatizing ones that followed, I try not to get too wrapped up in the importance of work. I try to remember that it's not my only purpose—I have a life with hobbies and interests and people who care about me without any monetary incentive whatsoever. I am not going to die for Burger King. I also try to remember that, even when employers say humanizing things like "We care about you," and "We're all one big work family," they're still referring to a family that pays me, which is what people used to call a "business." And a business just isn't equipped to fulfill all the complex needs of a thinking, feeling, multifaceted human being. They are far better at fulfilling their own life's purpose: making money. Personally, I can't let my happiness and self-worth depend on how good I am at making money—or on how some business lady named Karen is going to feel about squares.

My Life Has No Meaning, but Have You Tried the New Toaster?

DESPITE THE BUSINESS BEING OBSCENELY PROFITABLE, our office is overcrowded, we are underpaid, and our work almost certainly supports fracking, heart disease, and the blatant exploitation of the poor. In recent months, it has occurred to me that this makes what I do, at best, completely void of meaning and, at worst, totally amoral. In short, my life has no meaning, but . . . have you tried the new toaster?

Now, if you're thinking, "a toaster is not a good enough reason to continuing living such a futile existence," then you've never experienced the way a piece of golden-brown bread, gently rising from an evenly heated cooking chamber, can lift one's battered spirits from even the darkest pits of despair. To the truly downtrodden, those warm tendrils of steam feel like an approximation of love . . . $600 worth of bread-making love.

It's been a true epiphany realizing that it's not working sixteen-hour days and coming in on weekends that leaves me with an empty feeling inside, it's a lack of toasted carbohydrates! All of my true suffering has been at the hands of obsolete toasting technology, and the benevolence of upper management has now delivered me from that false breakfast prophet. Thanks to the fine specimen of modern kitchen convenience we received today, all of my former problems have been solved.

Other corporate sweatshops, I beseech you: Cast aside your shoddy spring-loaded toasting devices, for there is a machine that will smoothly lower thy employees' bread at the press of a button. It will change them. I used to think I should get paid overtime, but then I realized this thing has over ten different settings! Sure, I still lay awake at night thinking about how I make money for people who actively oppose climate change legislation, but who can sleep when you're this excited about making an English muffin in the morning?

Before the boon of the new toaster, I was considering finding a new, less soul-crushing job, but the heavenly aroma of warm bread is all I needed to forget the marked absence of hope that permeates my work environment. Don't worry, it's not your fault if you haven't seen the light yet—those glowing, orange strips of light that fill my heart with joy.

My suggestion is to stop searching for meaning in your work. The meaning of life is golden brown and waiting for you to butter it. Each morning, I witness a breakfast miracle, and with it comes new hope and new light. And light is exactly what I need right now, because office services just moved my desk into a storage closet. But whatever, because have you seen the new toaster?

Jobs I'm Actively Googling During Work Hours

IF YOU HAVE A STABLE OFFICE JOB THAT PAYS A LIVING wage, you probably know on an intellectual level that you're lucky. You know that most of the managers you report to directly were likely part of the workforce in 2008, survived the Great Recession, and therefore think you're an ungrateful troll for even saying the words "work-life balance." You even know that there are other people who would be happy to have your cushy desk job. But that doesn't mean you don't gaze longingly out of glass-walled conference rooms, dreaming about an alternate universe where you decide to become a large animal vet serving the farmers of the English countryside. It doesn't mean you don't zone out on client calls and fantasize about starting over as a professional beekeeper. In fact, a tiny piece of your soul dies for every second you spend staring into the cold void of your company-issued laptop, instead of foraging for mushrooms in an enchanting moss-covered forest—and by "you" I mean "me." Because these are the jobs I'm actively googling during work hours:

Park Ranger

When I'm web searching "jobs where you walk around outside all day"—instead of completing basic tasks like doing my timesheets—"park ranger" is always one of the first hits. It doesn't pay much, but can you really put a dollar value on living and working in some of America's most treasured natural landscapes? I'd probably still be required to do some dull administrative tasks, like reporting how many baby deer I saw that day, but at least I'd be an administrator of the forest. The only thing stopping me from quitting my spine-curling desk job and spending my days educating campers in the woods is at least twenty-four college credit hours in natural sciences, earth sciences, archeology, anthropology, museum sciences, public administration, park and recreation management, social sciences, or sociology—none of which I currently possess. It's obvious that going back to college and putting myself into more debt than I can easily repay on a park ranger salary isn't ideal, but at least I won't have HR constantly harassing me about those overdue timesheets anymore.

Shepherd

As I ignore my project manager's incessant reminders about my next deadline, I often find myself wondering, "Is shepherding even still a job?" Shockingly, yes! A little research reveals that you can still become a shepherd in some parts of the world. I like to imagine tending to my herd, a smattering of fluffy white specks on a bucolic green landscape of rolling hills. It would look just like my current desktop background. Although, the photographer may have left out some of the less idyllic scenes, such as retrieving rogue sheep that wander off and die in bogs, moving the herd over miles of snowy terrain with only the help of a dog, and the horrors of a ewe's prolapsed uterus in lambing season. Those minor details aside, all I have to do is work my way up from the bottom and gain years of practical hands-on experience doing hard labor for other people until I eventually save up enough money to afford my own meager tenancy. Then I can say goodbye to toiling away in a crowded open office and hello to toiling away in the muddy open fields.

Herbalist

It might be too late to catch up on whatever happened in my full-team internal regroup while I was scanning the internet for a new career, but it's never too late to become an herbalist. Some programs even offer remote learning, so I can take classes while continuing to pretend I care about what's going on at work. Just imagine how romantic my medicinal herb shop upstate will look with bundles of flowers drying in the windows, bowls of freshly foraged mushrooms on the counters, and shelves full of mysterious powders and tinctures covering the walls. Will growing and selling my own questionable herbal remedies be a viable business model in the long term? That's between me, the spirits of nature, and the lawyer who will be filing my Chapter 11. Speaking of the law, I won't legally be able to call myself a doctor, but there's nothing stopping me from calling myself a witch!

Gamekeeper

Did I look up this rare occupation when I should have had my nose to the grindstone like a good employee? Yes. Had I read one too many D. H. Lawrence novels at the time? Also, yes. Thanks to my research, though, I'm now aware that I may have to kill animals in this line of work, which seems highly unpleasant. Apparently it's not all hatching baby pheasants and seducing the lady of the estate in the charming gamekeeper's shed like I thought. You might actually have to hunt more game than you keep—and just keep it in your pants in general. To be absolutely sure, I'm going to look into it further the next time I'm certain no one can see my computer screen.

Beekeeper

What could be more peaceful than warm rays of sun filtering through golden jars of honey? Certainly not my nine-to-forever job as a capitalist worker drone. That's why I've pulled up at least fifty browser tabs about starting my own apiary on the rooftop of my apartment building. Sure, there's always a chance my hive could go rogue and swarm innocent people and halal carts down on the street, but it's a chance I'm willing to take. I'd unleash thousands of confused and agitated bees upon my neighbors if it meant never having to open an Excel spreadsheet again.

Country Vet

As I gaze out at the desk farm that drains energy from me and my fellow coworkers the way mechanized dairy farms drain milk from cows, I imagine what it would be like to work with actual dairy cows. According to the internet, I might need to know more than the most basic math to get through veterinary school, but think of all the cute fuzzy animals that would be my new coworkers. Plus, I'd spend my days driving across the rural countryside, going from picturesque farm to picturesque farm, like a modern James Herriot. Of course, James Herriot also regularly found himself buried up to the shoulder in various cow, horse, and sheep orifices, often before the sun was even up. I'll have to see if I still find the fuzzy animals cute from that vantage point, or if I'm even capable of waking up before 9 a.m.

Lumberjack

I looked this one up during a mandatory office happy hour because I was a little buzzed and I like flannel shirts. However, it quickly became clear that lumberjacks are not the whimsical caretakers of the forest I've seen portrayed in hipster culture. In its modern manifestation, lumberjacking is just mechanized tree mass murder. I can't go around rejecting the principles of corporate America on moral grounds, only to turn around and become the bad guy from *FernGully*. This one is off the table.

Homesteader

At this point, I'm so burned out that I don't really care if anyone catches me watching hours and hours of homesteading YouTube videos on company time. I've finally reached the only valid conclusion that will allow me to quit my job, start over, and drop out of capitalism all together: I must become a homesteader. I'll just need to learn to grow my own food, sew my own clothes, tend my own chickens, milk my own goats, make my own candles, dig my own well, and build my own log cabin by hand somewhere off the grid. This is it, though, the answer to all my modern angst. I'm going to stick it to the man by living off the land—the only way to truly escape the system—and I'm going to do it just as soon as I feel comfortable giving up my steady paycheck, job stability, contributions to my 401(k), access to company healthcare, and Free Pizza Fridays. So, any day now, really. Any. Day. Now.

The Ten Commandments of Workism

I.   I am the Lord thy Job, who brought thee out of the land of unemployment, out of the house of bondage to thy parents. Thou shalt not have family, friends, romantic relationships, hobbies, or outside interests before me. Thou shalt not make to thyself a life, nor the likeness of a life, for I am a jealous Job, hating them that sin against me and bestowing mercy on them that love me and keep my commandments.

II.   Thou shalt not take the name of the Lord thy Job in vain. Not in the lobby, not in the elevator, not in the hallway, not at thy desk, not in the breakroom, and certainly not in online forums designed to hold employers accountable for how they treat and/or compensate their employees.

III.   Remember to keep holy the Sabbath day. Five days thou shalt labor and one day thou shalt go to the farmers market, seek sexual intercourse, or do laundry as thou pleaseth. But the seventh day is the Sabbath and on this day thou shalt receive emails from thy supervisor that apparently couldn't possibly wait until Monday morning. For in the beginning, Job the Father created a positive net profit in six days and divided it amongst the Partners and the CEOs and the Executive Directors, and on the seventh day he rested very uneasily with a sense of creeping dread at the prospect of laboring once more. Therefore, he blessed the seventh day so that thou might feel this dread as well. Except for Karen, who will rejoice and flood the inboxes of every coworker on earth and in heaven.

IV.   Honor thy mother and thy father, for it was them that cosigned the student loans that will forever hold thee financially hostage in the Kingdom of Capitalism.

V.   Thou shalt not commit adultery by taking interviews with other Jobs. Thou hast but one true Job, thy Shepherd, and no real identity outside of His flock. And what if other Jobs don't have free snacks and a beer cart on Friday like thine?

VI.   Thou shalt not steal pens or paper clips, printer paper or ink, and certainly not precious time. Every minute spent looking at thy phone in a bathroom stall is a minute stolen. Every sick day is a day pilfered. Every moment not spent eating, sleeping, or working at thy desk is a larceny committed. Thy time is thy Job's time. Thou shalt rise and grind each day unceasingly until death takes thee or HR terminates thee.

VII.   Thou shalt not kill. Unless it has been specifically stipulated in thy contract or is required to achieve an IPO.

VIII.   Thou shalt not bear false witness against thy coworker. Steve probably did not mean to touch thy breast by the photocopier. Also, HR would like to know why thy breasts were made so readily available for touching in the first place.

IX.   Thou shalt not covet thy coworker's salary. Thou shalt not even ask thy coworker to name it and thou absolutely shalt not give it to Glassdoor.com. Thou shalt be satisfied with thy monetary blessings and cease repeatedly asking for a raise. The heavenly employer has already explained multiple times that it is not a good time financially, even though we just went public, and it's very complicated and hard to explain in layman's terms. Thou simply wouldn't understandeth.

X.   Thou shalt not covet thy coworker's work-life balance, nor their healthy attitude toward using vacation time, nor their ability to eat lunch away from their desk, nor their friendships with people outside the office, nor their many interesting hobbies, nor the love of their family, which they insist on making time for even though it's incredibly unprofitable. Have faith that thy one true Job will see the sins of such a coworker and fire them to the flaming depths of workism hell.

Instead, oh holiest of worshippers, covet nothing but the short-lived, cheap imitation of meaningful fulfillment and realized identity bestowed upon the followers of the holy trinity: The Work, The Work, and The Holy Work. Then, one day, thou shalt submit thy sacred timesheet and ascend to labor eternally in the Kingdom of heavenly profit, a blessed child of Job.

Praise be to work!

Anything Men Can Do
I Can Do Bleeding

HELLO, CIS MEN! I THOUGHT THIS WOULD BE A GOOD time to remind you that anything you can do, I can do bleeding. That's right, whatever it is you did today, I can probably do it while hemorrhaging from the most sensitive part of my body. And I won't die! Remember that when you're standing on the train in the morning surrounded by bodies—roughly half of them female bodies. They could be bleeding. Standing and bleeding. Walking and bleeding. Smiling and bleeding.

Think about it. A mortal being, walking the earth, shedding her blood continuously for a week, all while looking totally normal and smiling through eight hours of continuous meetings to avoid workplace discrimination. And the whole amazing process is partially controlled by the gravitational patterns of the moon. That's right—my body is controlled by a giant space rock. A floating rock in the depths of space decides when I bleed. I think nine out of ten horror movie writers would agree that this alone makes me about one mutation shy of needing to be killed with a stake.

Now, you're probably thinking that all this bleeding must be detrimental to my work. After all, humans need their blood to make spreadsheets and eat salads and attend internal debriefings. Well, you would be wrong. Dead wrong. You know what isn't dead though? Me after bleeding constantly for seven days.

Remember that meeting yesterday? The one where you talked over me repeatedly, so that I was forced to yell over you? It was so fun, both of us yelling like that. Weren't you pumped? I was so pumped, but I was also pumping blood out of my uterus. That's right, my life force was being pumped out of my body and into my pants—my fashionable, androgynous business pants. Sure, that meeting was high stakes for you, but just one sneeze and it would've been all over for me. Seriously, it would've been all over my very expensive pants.

So what if you negotiated the big deal and signed the huge contract? Did you sign your huge contract in blood? No, you didn't, because you're not a blood machine like me. Everyone knows that a contract is never more legally binding than when it's been sealed with a bodily fluid. What fluids do you have on hand? Only clear ones? How embarrassing for you.

Oh, and it's not just at the office that I can get things done while leaving a trail of blood in my wake. You should see me at the public swimming pool. They say men and women aren't athletically matched, but how many men train for their intramural city swim meets in the open ocean with blood-seeking sharks? None that would have to worry about the blood-seeking part!

Men, what I'm saying is this: You may have the upper hand right now, but never forget—anything you can do I can do bleeding. That is, just as soon as I take this aspirin and muster the strength to get up off the couch.

Which Hallmark Movie Job Will Get You Your Happy Ending?

IF YOU'VE WATCHED MORE THAN ONE HALLMARK MOVIE, you've probably noticed that the heroines tend to work in the same few industries in every film. It's a lot of baking, nurturing, marketing, and shopkeeping. This could be due to gender norms, audience appeal, or the will of the computer AI that generates the scripts. Or it could be that these specific careers are the true key to living your most perfect made-for-TV-movie life. Perhaps a Hallmark movie job is just what you need to achieve the sexless, whitewashed, computer-generated happily ever after of your dreams. The only question is, which of these careers is right for you?

Bakery Owner

The cutest of all Hallmark heroine jobs. It's particularly great if you can see yourself as the strictly regimented baker who needs to learn how to let loose and have fun, or the starry-eyed manic pixie cupcake maker who is always covered in flour. Either way, you're going to be pastel, adorable, and looking for love. Keep an eye out for that one guy in a tight-fitting sweater who likes to tease you for seemingly no reason and needs you to make three hundred cupcakes by Friday for his big business thing. You'll probably hate

him at first, but that's just your lackluster chemistry building—
don't you know that teasing is how emotionally repressed men
tell you they like you? He's going to end up helping you in the
kitchen, and things are going to heat up fast when you get icing
all over his Men's Wearhouse pullover. That'll be your cue to really
set the mood and tell him about your dead mom. All you remember about her is that she loved spaghetti and you made cupcakes
together. You named the bakery after her, and Mr. Business
Casual is all too happy to listen to your dreams of launching a
special cupcake in her honor. Will anyone like your experimental
spaghetti-flavored dead mom cupcakes? It doesn't really matter as
long as you and your knight in pleated khakis continue to uphold
thinly veiled Christian values, the Western nuclear family ideal,
and a commitment to kissing without tongues.

Big-City Lawyer

A great choice for the ambitious type. You can prove just how
smart and successful you are before giving it all up to work on
a ranch with your new cowboy love interest. Yep, that's right,
you're not staying in the big city for long. I mean, you could just
be a high-powered lawyer living a luxurious urban lifestyle, but
wouldn't you rather be happy? After all, the law is the only thing
more boring than numbers. That's why you're going to ditch that
big important job for the first man you see whispering gently to
a horse. Thanks to your legal expertise, you're going to be in the
perfect position to help this square-jawed cowhand settle a long-
standing property dispute. No, not a dispute over the fact that he
inherited his property from ancestors who probably stole it from
Indigenous peoples, but over his neighbor's claim that the ranch's
famous BBQ stand encroaches on his property. All you have to
do to achieve your happy ending is avoid frantic calls from your

concerned coworkers, win your cowboy's case, and endure an endless gag reel of everything from BBQ sauce to horse manure getting flung at your pristine tailored silk suits.

Something Vaguely in Marketing

This is the gig for you if you just want to shuffle some papers around and say the words "big presentation" every five to ten minutes. The exact thing you do within marketing isn't important. You just vaguely come up with the campaigns to increase the sales to win the business and beat the competition. Until, of course, you find yourself in a charming mountain town for the holidays, probably because your car broke down on the way to the big pitch meeting or whatever. This is your opportunity to bump into a taciturn lumberjack loner who doesn't approve of your slick sales-pitching ways. Fortunately, this prickly plaid daddy is going to realize he needs you the moment he overhears you give some truly revolutionary advice to the local cafe owner. Creating a social media profile for their business? Genius! That's when he knows you're the key to saving his failing family-owned ski lodge. So, go ahead and use that advertising savant brain of yours to make a truly groundbreaking brochure. How would they ever have thought to market a family-owned ski lodge to families without your help? When you're ready to seal the deal with Lumberjack Ken™, look at him with your best doe eyes and whisper, "I've never seen snow before." He'll propose on the spot, and you can start your life together in ski chalet paradise.

Journalist

The most popular Hallmark heroine job. If all you want is a bit of forced proximity with a male celebrity, then a career in

journalism might be for you. The list of successful yet troubled
bachelors your boss could demand you interview is practically
endless. You could get assigned to a broken-hearted country
music star or a troubled tech billionaire, but why not go for
the gold standard of Hallmark celebrity: a prince! Specifically,
the crown prince of Schmaldovia, a tiny European-ish country
nestled somewhere between Schmitaly and Schmance along
the snowy Schmalps mountain range. Unfortunately, the prince
doesn't give interviews. That's why—to get the real scoop on
the upcoming Schmaldovian coronation—you hatch a plan to
work undercover as a maid in his palace. What you didn't plan
on was falling in love with this bland-as-white-bread slice of
man at first sight, and him falling in love with you, his supposed
employee, right back. Questionable power dynamics aside, your
love proves to be very distracting. When you look back at your
spy notes, you'll find that all you've written is "Why prince not
want crown?" "Prince looks handsome in crown." "Can't find
Schmaldovia on map?" By the time your editor reads the gar-
bled mess of a piece you've sent him, you'll have almost entirely
forgotten that you're a journalist at all. You'll be so close with
the prince that you'll have helped him deal with his mommy
issues, saved a local orphanage together, and suggested sweeping
legislative changes to the government of Schmaldovia, all while
pretending to be a humble housekeeper who sees the real him.
Once you and the Prince of Wonderbread reconcile over your
itsy-bitsy minor deception of being an undercover journalist,
it's only a short horseback ride to princess town for you. Screw
journalism—the only things you'll be writing from now on are
royal decrees, and possibly a tell-all when your marriage falls
apart due to a rushed engagement, the pressures of royal life, and
your relationship being based on a lie. This is still technically a

happy ending because you're going to do really well in the divorce settlement.

Event Planner

Just the thing to set you on your path to fulfillment—if you identify as Type A, have an almost pathological need for organization, and believe that most problems in life can be solved with a single trip to Michaels. Normally this line of work would require something of an artistic eye, but we're talking about the Hallmark movie version of event planning, so really you could do this with your eyes closed. Just follow some basic rules for every event and you'll be golden:

1. Make a banner stating the name and/or theme of the event.
2. Cover everything in string lights.
3. Use a ladder. Clumsily falling off them is a great way to find a man.

Now that you have the tools to do the job, get ready to meet the tool you're going to do—off-screen, after you're married, and only for procreative purposes. He's Mr. Type B, the most relaxed chill guy ever to go with the flow. Despite the fact that you're paying him to work on your latest event—a large formal wedding—he'll disrupt your plans, mock your no-nonsense attitude, and propose a bet that you can't possibly sit back and relax for one week. You know, because you're soooooo uptight. If you win the bet, he'll use his handyman skills to build the elaborate, heart-shaped arbor your caricature of a bride wants for her wedding day, free of charge. If he wins, you must admit that your whole personality is wrong and bad and allow him to crush your independent spirit. Not to be beaten by this roguish layabout, you'll make several comical attempts to be laid-back—you'll even wear your hair down! But, oddly enough, it seems like your new attitude might actually be detrimental to your job. It's almost like you got hired to plan this wedding *because* you're so intensely put together and meticulous. Who cares about job security or taking pride in your work though? Because the chillest guy on Earth has started to fall for you now that you're less . . . you. By the end of the week, you and your handsome slacker are going to be well on your way to sharing a life of Hallmark happiness.

Something Real Estate Adjacent

This is the ultimate calling for those who truly cherish home—or houses. Whether you sell them, flip them, or architect them isn't really important. What's important is that your current love interest/business partner does not understand your dreams for the future of your home-selling/flipping/architecting business. He cares more about the money than the craft. Fortunately, a new love interest just strolled into your open house, and though he may be dumber than a bag of hammers, he understands your passion. He encourages you to take the professional risks you've been weighing carefully for so long, mostly because he lacks any business sense whatsoever. It's just the push you needed to finally end your toxic relationship and pursue your passion for custom doorknobs and popcorn ceilings. Sure, you might not have a lifetime of scintillating conversation to look forward to with your handsome cheerleader, but at least he doesn't spend 95 percent of his time taking poorly timed phone calls and storming out of rooms like your ex. Not to mention, everything you do together is so much fun, even filing for bankruptcy on your popcorn ceiling and doorknob business.

Farmer (Preferably a Seasonal One)

Farming is by far the most picturesque of the Hallmark heroine jobs; there's no industrial agriculture going on here. This farm is more of a glorified vegetable patch where you grow only pumpkins. Unfortunately, the extremely seasonal pumpkin business has been failing for the last couple of years and some developers are pressuring you to sell the land. Things might seem dire now, but this could be your ideal career if you believe in all that "pull yourself up by your bootstraps" stuff. Lucky for you, there's someone in town who has been eyeing your bootstraps for a while. His struggling farm is right next door to yours, and he grows exclusively Christmas trees. You two used to date in high school, but ever since you dumped him at the town pumpkin festival years ago, he's had an aversion to all things fall. To really compound the trauma, you also recently found out that you were adopted and your biological parents died in a tragic Christmas tree decorating accident. What are the odds? In an act of true bravery, your Christmas Tree Farmer will confess that he's been pining for you all this time, and—if you're willing to set aside your fear of murderous evergreens—he'll be willing to work through his autumnal pumpkin trauma. You both want to learn to trust again, so you'll agree to join forces and thwart the evil developers. Obviously, you're going to give your romance a second chance and learn to appreciate the beauty of each other's seasonal agricultural endeavors, just in time to save both farms. You'll also invent your own seasonal drink for the transitional time between fall and winter and call it the peppermint pumpkin mocha spice latte. It's made with milk, espresso, chocolate syrup, whole peppermints, and a heaping scoop of raw pumpkin. It's going to win first prize at the very specific Right Between Winter and Fall Festival your town holds every year, and a Starbucks executive will just happen to be there to witness it. They'll buy the rights to the recipe, and you'll live happily ever after off the royalty checks.

Writer

Now this career, though it's a bit clichéd, is another frequently seen Hallmark movie job that guarantees profound happiness and a perfect—wait.

Where is my Hallmark happy ending?!

Have You Tried Buying Things?

ON EXPENSIVE CUPS, OVERPRICED
FACE CREAMS, FANCY UNDERWEAR, AND
OTHER ATTEMPTS TO BUY HAPPINESS.

Have You Tried Buying Artisanal Glassware?

ON AN AVERAGE DAY, THERE ARE AT LEAST ONE OR TWO moments where I feel pulled toward a potential depressive spiral. For this reason, like many people, I have developed coping mechanisms to steer me away from those beckoning pits of despair. Not today, "urge to dwell on the fact that death is inevitable," we're going to look at some trees instead! Unfortunately, I don't think anyone was fully prepared to cope with the internal chaos that arises from a global pandemic and endless months of mandatory lockdown. Least of all myself.

After various unsuccessful attempts at filling the ever-growing void threatening to swallow me whole on a daily basis, I had a truly brilliant thought: What about stuff? Could buying stuff be the solution to these uncomfortable feelings? Could possessing objects make me feel like a whole well-adjusted person? Maybe stuff and things would furnish the emptiness within me and put a damper on that voice in my head saying, "You've wasted your youth on a soulless career," and "Bangs are a great idea!" Maybe I should listen to the barrage of marketing telling me to "make your home a sanctuary in these trying times." Maybe what I've really needed my whole life wasn't purpose or human connection, but a set of handmade-to-order sacred art objects sculpted from epiphany glass—in layman's terms, cute little cups.

The cups I'm referring to were shown to me by a friend with very good taste and a penchant for finding the most expensive one-of-a-kind I-met-the-artist-when-I-picked-it-up kind of items. They are the type of person who buys original artwork, something that is unfathomable to me as a print-buying peasant (though they would want me to clarify that they are not exceedingly wealthy, just somewhat whimsical when it comes to managing money). When they showed me these cups, every rational thought I've ever had about fiscal responsibility evaporated from my brain. All that was left was unchecked desire and cups. They were spun from glass and about four inches tall. Each one was a sort of tulip shape with the kind of wobbly-edged imperfections that let you know they weren't stamped from a mechanical mold on a factory assembly line. They were mostly white with watercolor-esque splashes of mint green, bright yellow, lavender, and flamingo pink. Imagine the cast of *Miami Vice* did a few lines and went to a paint-your-own pottery place, but in a good way. I thought about them for days, especially as I was trying to avoid more unpleasant thoughts, like "How much longer will I be stuck sitting alone in my apartment?" and "Why did I decide to live so far away from all my friends and family?" and "Could that tickle in the back of my throat be the beginning of the end?" As I faced the disappointing hodgepodge of discount glassware in my kitchen cupboard early one morning—the one Zoom-free part of my day—I couldn't take it anymore. I had to have the cups.

I did ask my friend some questions before rushing headlong into a purchase. Not the important ones, like "How much did these cost?" and "Are they dishwasher safe?" but rather "What does one drink from a four-inch-tall cup?" Their answer: Wine? Perhaps a cocktail? Your customary glass of OJ as part of a complete breakfast? Good enough for me. These would now be the fanciest wine/cocktail/juice cups I'd ever owned. I fantasized about having them in my possession for years to come. Other people would have stories about their children to share in their old age; I would have the story of my magnificent epiphany glass cups. Wine would somehow taste better when sipped from their delightfully irregular rims. A $15 red blend from Kroger would morph into a $50 Pinot Noir from a local biodynamic winery the moment it touched their handblown glass sides. I imagined the compliments I would get from future guests as I presented them with drinks, forgetting that I was a shut-in pond witch who counts "letting Animal Control in to catch the squirrel in my living room wall" as "hosting a soirée." These cups would, without a doubt, fill the yawning chasm in my chest longing for something more. So, I set out to acquire them.

I thought I could order the cups from the glass artist's website, but my fancy friend insisted on putting me in touch with the owner of the eclectic bespoke art items shop where they'd bought their own set. You see, the shop owner had a good relationship with the cup artist, who made the special tulip-shaped ones just for her. She would later explain to me that the other shapes and styles available on the artist's website were the ones he also sold to *dramatic pause* West Elm. Gods of Capitalism forbid I should have ended up with something so common as to be available at West Elm. A narrow miss, really.

In the capable hands of the shop owner—let's call her Margot—I explained exactly what I wanted: a set of four cups, white ones with splashes of bright color like my friend's set. We looked at sample photos, we discussed the craftsmanship, and we agreed that we both knew exactly what I was after.

Margot had, serendipitously, just put in a request with the cup artist, who we will henceforth refer to as "The Glass

Whisperer." She told me that he was, at that precise moment, delicately coaxing into existence from the divine fires of his workshop the very type of magical drinkware I'd described. But she would call him up and relay my wishes anyway, just to be safe. "He can be a little temperamental and . . . uh . . . unpredictable sometimes. You know, when inspiration strikes." I was too drunk on the imaginary wine flowing from visions of life-changing made-to-order sacred art objects to see the waving red flag in that sentence. What could possibly go wrong when working with a mercurial, glass-smithing wizard man?

A few weeks later, Margot messaged me with the long-awaited news. A fresh batch of cups were in, hot off the—weird poky glass-making tongs? She included a picture of a single cup at the bottom of her message, an incomplete preview of what was to come. As I scrolled down, I wondered what ownable art I'd be getting for my collection. What swirling pastel combinations would make my fantasy "Golden Girls at the MoMA" color palette come true? But when I came to the bottom of the message, I did not find the drinking vessel of my dreams. Sure, it was the right size and shape, but the color palette—words will never truly do it justice.

Nothing has ever embodied the term "eyesore" so well as this cup. At first glance, it appeared to be a pastel shade of lavender with murky splotches of red and yellow, rimmed with black and brown, the shades reminiscent of what happens when a kid takes an "all the colors at once" approach to finger painting. Upon closer inspection, I realized the purple base wasn't completely uniform. It had a subtle ombre effect, going from bluish purple at the bottom to almost pink at the rim. The splotches were the real issue though. They had the look and feel of bad abstract art—the kind of thing you might find on the walls of a dated hotel chain, or in the home decor bargain bin at Stein Mart. But the best description of these splotches? "Fish Lips," a Kaffe Fassett fabric pattern beloved by quilters the world over that looks somewhere between psychedelic nightmare fungi and what you see when you observe malaria under a microscope. Looking at the photo Margot had sent me, all I could see were Fish Lips.

It is probably clear at this point that I am an anxious person. I don't hate social interactions by any means, but I do constantly wonder if I'm doing them right. So, sometimes I go along with things I know might be detrimental to me and my mental health in the long term purely for the sake of avoiding discomfort in the short term. That is why my response to Margot and her shipment of extremely ugly cups was "I can't wait to see them in person :)." Please imagine that smile emoticon with the deadest of ten-thousand-yard stares.

Knowing full well that I hated the cup she'd shown me, I scheduled a time to meet Margot at her shop and pick up my set of four. You see, if I had backed out, Margot might've told my fancy friend what a faithless no-show I'd turned out to be. She might've told them that I'd led her on for weeks and then never followed through with a purchase. Why did I imagine Margot as a high school boy in an '80s teen movie trying to pressure his girlfriend into sex? All I can say is it's very hard to be in my brain sometimes.

I did, however, harbor some small hope that the other cups would be different from the one I'd seen in the photo. Weren't they all supposed to be completely unique, artisanal, not necessarily matching? These unseen mystery cups could be everything I'd ever wanted, or at least not covered in fish lips. I told myself this beautiful lie for several days, right up until I began the hour-long walk from my house to the shop. That's when I panicked. I texted my three closest friends to confess what I'd done. They of course responded with the only reasonable things one can say in this situation:

- You said you'd buy four cups? Well, how much are they?
- The price isn't listed?! You know that's not good, right?
- So, you absolutely hated the first cup and you're going to look at the rest anyway?
- Don't buy the cups.
- Please don't buy the cups.
- No, not even just two of them.
- You can do this. Do this for me. Do NOT buy these cups.

After a phone call with one friend, in which we discussed the inherent irrationality of buying things strictly out of guilt and wrongly perceived social obligation, I marched into Margot's shop with confidence. And immediately saw ten identical purple cups covered in fish lips waiting on a little table just for me. My eyes met Margot's over the top of our face masks, and I felt my confidence wither. I continued to quietly die inside as she explained that she'd just opened her small storefront in March, right before we all went into COVID-19 lockdown. "Wow! Crazy timing," I said, exuding the manic energy of a wild animal with its leg caught in a trap. As we made small talk about the benefits of masks and the precarious future of her small business, I frantically scanned the store for something else to buy. Anything but those cups.

Surely, she must sell one other useful item. One thing I could justify buying to get out of the shop guilt-free. One shelf held a green paper-mache dog sculpture. Another had what appeared to be two kissing birds made of wicker. There were painted wall masks, thumb-sized wooden bowls, and a stack of clay turtles. I was surrounded by tchotchkes, with not one single practical object in sight, and not one visible price tag.

Out of options, I was forced to muster my courage and make an attempt at honesty. I hesitantly said, "To be honest, these cups aren't quite what I was expecting . . ." Even that lame half-hearted protest was enough to send a panicked rush of adrenaline through my body, but for a moment I thought I might just escape unscathed.

"Oh yeah," Margot said. "The Glass Whisperer can be a little . . . capricious at times. I never really know what I'm going to get. Seems like he got stuck on perfecting this one pattern, ha! I totally understand if you only want to buy two right now." Those last words, "if you only want to buy two right now." They were the final blow from an experienced salesperson who could spot weakness like mine from a mile away. Two hideous cups were her price for a clean exit.

As she continued to talk about how much she loved the cups, I started to think maybe I'd been wrong about them. Maybe the longer I looked at them, the more I'd start to like them. Maybe these cups were a Dadaist masterpiece and I just didn't under-stand them yet because the joke was on me, the consumer.

Caught squarely between the shame of having to tell Margot I wouldn't be buying any cups and the shame of having to tell my friends that I'd bought a whole set, I selected a single cup— Margot's favorite, in fact. She said the splotches on it reminded her of flower petals. Probably because that's what she, the true cup artist, intended for them to look like when she hastily threw them together the previous night in the backroom of her shop. Flower petals? Clearly she's never seen Fish Lips. "That will be $70," Margot said, reaching for my credit card.

On my walk home, my cup of shame felt like it would burn a hole through its little paper bag. I called one of my friends to admit that I'd folded like a card table. It was obvious I was hoping for some absolution, and she kindly agreed that I'd done my best. While crossing a bridge, I considered tossing the cup over the side. Fish Lips belonged at the bottom of a river, didn't they? I could pretend this had never happened. But I could not in good conscience throw a $70 cup off a bridge. Maybe I could give it to someone? Like my worst enemy.

I decided to keep the cup buried deep in the back of my closet until the end of the pandemic, possibly until the end of time. I can't drink from it without reliving my embarrassment, but I also can't justify getting rid of something so absurdly expensive. Instead, it haunts me like the telltale heart of retail humiliation, reminding me of that time I tried to fill the void with artisanal glassware. The irony of looking for fulfillment from an object that is itself an empty vessel is not lost on me. And so, my recommendation is this: If you're going to try to ease your loneliness or looming sense of existential emptiness with "stuff," at the very least, pick something that is less hollow than you.

Five Extremely Expensive Rugs That Will Definitely Solve All Your Problems

THEY SAY THAT THE RIGHT RUG CAN CHANGE YOUR entire living space, but an expensive rug can change your entire life. All you have to do is obsessively scour the internet day and night for the perfect pile of costly handwoven fibers to transform your mundane existence into the home decor fantasy of your choosing. Just scroll manically through countless colors, shapes, and sizes, slowly developing an involuntary eye twitch, until you find a patterned strip of material that simultaneously floods your brain with decor-based delusions and drains your bank account dry. There's a plethora of prohibitively expensive styles to make your rug-related fantasies come true.

The Minimalist Rug

A neutral solid-colored rug can sometimes be the best blank canvas on which to project your aspirational musings. Allow the minimalist aesthetic to carry you off into a fantasy world where you just sold your billion-dollar start-up idea: Bluetooth shower caps for dogs! Imagine spending your days as the queen of disruptive dog hygiene products in your neutral-toned haven where nothing has color and everything has hairpin legs. Picture yourself reclining on your gray sectional couch, under your cream-colored alpaca throw, in your navy cashmere loungewear set, by the light of an arced brass floor lamp. You're probably writing thank-you notes to your angel investors, mom and dad. In this world, stains don't exist, spills never happen, and clutter evaporates on contact with surfaces. Sometimes you drink red wine over the dry-clean-only ivory tufts of your rug just to get a quick hit of the adrenaline you once felt launching your start-up, but that's as close as you get to risk these days. This minimalist fantasy could exist outside of your head if you'd just order that obscenely expensive ivory wool rug you've been eyeing for weeks. Whatever you do, though, don't be fooled by cheap synthetic look-alikes that promise the same aesthetic for less. You may think IKEA sells a similar rug in the same shade of Champagne Dreams Ivory, but for several hundred dollars less it's probably more like Sweat-Stained T-shirt Beige. At least, that's how it'll start to look once you've obsessively compared it to the more expensive rug for hours on end.

The Mid-Century Modern Rug

Who hasn't occasionally wished we could all return to the simpler times of the 1950s? Well, maybe those of us who aren't straight cisgender white men, but surely everyone else has wished it at least once. All you need to transport yourself to a world of midday martinis and indoor smoking is an extravagant area rug with a large modern geometric pattern. Let the striking shapes and bold colors stoke your fantasies of hosting elaborate dinner parties for your husband's boss by night and vacuuming your rug in a Valium-induced haze by day. Pretend you have a white picket fence, a tennis club membership, and no idea that cigarettes cause cancer. In this fantasy, you don't have to work, so your only real problem is Betty Friedan's "problem that has no name." But who cares? You get to watch soaps all day and take speed legally in the form of diet pills. You could make this retro lifestyle your reality if only you'd forget about frugality and order yourself an over-priced mid-century modern rug from an online-only millennial furniture retailer. You won't regret it, just like no one in the '50s ever regretted prescribing lobotomies or driving cars without seat belts.

The Sheepskin Rug

Legend tells us the Scandinavian concept of hygge—a quality of coziness that creates a sense of well-being—started when an eleventh-century Viking brutally hacked apart an adorable little sheep and used it to warm his cold Viking toes. So, if you want to properly immerse yourself in a Scandinavian hygge fantasy, you absolutely must spend this month's rent on the largest sheepskin you can find. Before you know it, you'll be sipping cocoa in a Fair Isle sweater with your Viking boyfriend Skarde the Spine Crusher at your side. That's right, you don't live in a 500-square-foot, fourth-floor apartment anymore; you live in the sturdy Viking yurt Skarde built for you with his own two hands—the same hands he uses to crush the spines of men and sheep alike. Disappear into this rugged yet comfy fantasy where you elaborately braid your hair every day and sip nourishing cups of broth while watching snow fall outside. Braid your hair, braid Skarde's hair, even braid the sheepskin rug's hair. Everything about your life is perfect and hairy and comfortable now. All it required was an irresponsible sum of money and the deaths of many cute docile grazing animals. You can't buy happiness, but you can buy hygge.

The Kilim Rug

The flat-weaving technique used to make these rugs produces crisp lines and bold patterns that will make you want to say, "Should we burn sage or palo santo tonight?" Why buy tickets to Coachella when you could buy a kilim rug and live out an overpriced desert-inspired fantasy at home instead? Disappear into a cactus-covered mirage where you're no longer you—you're you with a rudimentary understanding of yoga and seven fully cleansed chakras. Although they aren't yet spiritually cleansed—that takes a lot of work—just the kind of cleansed you get from drinking too much green juice and eating adaptogenic mushroom gummy vitamins all day. Still, you live a surreal life, dripping in the colors of a Joshua Tree sunset, surrounded by succulents, and adorned with magical healing crystals. It's so beautiful you'd almost think you were hallucinating, like that time you took ayahuasca and threw up your $20 macronutrient micro-greens salad all over the sacred geodesic dome. Your dreams of living in a bleached-cow-skull-and-macramé-covered oasis could be real, though, if only you'd stop hesitating and default on your student loans to buy yourself this gorgeous rug.

The Antique Persian Rug

Finally, we come to a mysterious yet scholarly fantasy for those with truly expensive taste. If you have a penchant for period-piece aesthetics and an unspoken desire to live in a gothic mansion with a woman locked in the attic, an antique Persian rug is the way to go. Let the fine vintage fibers sweep you into the moody world of crackling fireplaces, classical literature, and mist-covered moors. Just imagine walking down long, carpeted hallways in your white linen nightgown carrying a three-armed candelabra you thrifted on Etsy to investigate a strange noise coming from your library. It's probably just the ghost of a melancholic woman who drowned herself in the 1850s after daring to think about premarital sex. But there's always a chance it's a handsome man—who has perfectly justifiable reasons for locking women in attics—brooding over his undying love for you. As you tumble headfirst into this gothic reverie, don't forget to read some Lord Byron, commission a cursed oil painting of yourself, and buy a new wardrobe full of tweed blazers, turtleneck sweaters, and plaid skirts. Can't you just see yourself alone in your study with your books, your dark secrets, and your many overlapping antique Persian rugs? For mere hundreds of thousands of pennies, you could be living out this fantasy for the rest of your tortured intellectual life. All you have to do is give in to the call of compulsive shopping and buy that rug.

Now, you might be thinking, "Is it really worth it? Will a rug really make my life anything like these elaborate fantasies I've constructed in my head?" Of course it will! And please stop asking such silly questions. Because a rug is so much more than a beautiful piece of home decor. A rug is an investment—one that collects all the spills, crumbs, dirt, and dust people track through your home on a daily basis with their weird, gross, icky feet.

My Targeted Instagram Ads, Translated

THANKS TO THE HIGHLY PERSONAL NATURE OF INSTAGRAM collecting and selling my data to advertisers for profit, it can often feel like my targeted Instagram ads are speaking directly to me. Here's what I imagine they're saying:

Online Mattress Company Ad: One mattress fits all. Delivered right to your door.
Translation: If you don't buy a mattress from an online store, you'll have to go to a physical mattress store and interact with a living, breathing human sales representative. I think we both know you're not going to do that.

Bedding Ad: A better world starts with a better bed. Introducing the lived-in linen collection.
Translation: You cannot keep hooking up with people on sheets your mother purchased for you ten years ago at Pottery Barn Teen. They passed the "lived-in" stage a long time ago and are well on their way to looking "died-in."

Makeup Ad: It's time for clean beauty that naturally reveals the real you.

Translation: You must wear makeup even when you're going for the "no makeup" look. Now with slightly less poison than the previous formula!

Dress Ad: Honor Mother Earth in the Maribel Dress made from 100 percent flax linen.
Translation: We've noticed you follow a lot of urban farming accounts, which means you're either barely suppressing a *Little House on the Prairie* role-play fantasy, or you're on the verge of joining a commune led by a charismatic spiritual leader. Either way, you're going to need this flowing floral farm-to-fiber ankle-length dress. That'll be $300 please.

Furniture Ad: Great style is easy with these beautiful mid-century designs.
Translation: Buy your grandparents' furniture, but at half the quality and ten times the price. Isn't it crazy how, back then, they owned both pre-assembled particleboard-free furniture *and* their own home? You'll be lucky if you can afford this one tiny end table.

Another Dress Ad: From the earth, fashion blooms. Meet the new Meadow Dress!
Translation: We saw that you liked that other dress ad from before. It was probably just an accidental finger tap while scrolling, but that's not going to stop us from bombarding your feed with even more gauzy white linen. Don't you want to be as soft and feminine as these beautiful long-haired women frolicking through wildflowers and grassy meadows? Look at how our styles transform them into sultry milkmaids and sexy shepherdesses—they'll definitely look the same on you. There's absolutely zero

chance that in your real, non-Instagram life they'll look more like Jane Austen cosplay. Spend the $300 now.

Soup Meal Plan Subscription Ad: Subscribe to the Scintillating Spoon meal plan today and get one week of free soup.
Translation: We're not saying you should be on a diet, but have you considered only eating soup for weeks at a time? Food studies we paid for show that our soup-based meal plan might even be enough calories to keep you alive.

Disruptive Sneaker Brand Ad: Meet your new go-to sneakers.
Translation: If you work for a tech start-up, you are legally obligated to buy these shoes. If you're not a member of the aforementioned target market, please disregard.

Grain-Free Breakfast Cereal Ad: Healthy cereal so good you won't believe it's good for you.
Translation: It seems like the wellness industry has probably ruined your ability to enjoy a lot of foods you used to love, like cereal, so try our fad-diet-compliant version of Fruit Loops, Reese's Puffs, and Cinnamon Toast Crunch. We added protein, then removed the sugar, the carbs, and the joy, which means there's no reason to hate yourself for eating it!

Jewelry Ad: You don't need an occasion for fine jewelry anymore.
Translation: We can tell from your data patterns that you're probably not getting out much these days, but that doesn't mean you can't still bedeck yourself in jewels. That's right, you don't need a special occasion or a life milestone to justify buying jewelry anymore. Just order a diamond ring, throw on a ball gown, and sit at home like a modern Miss Havisham whenever the mood—or

targeted ad campaign—strikes you. You deserve to lounge in what our brand strategists are calling "tragic luxury," and we deserve your money.

Chiropractic Tool Ad: Relieve back pain fast with the Spine Wheel 3000. It's ten times as effective as a foam roller and it almost won on *Shark Tank.*
Translation: If two years of physical therapy, multiple massage therapists, various heating pads, regular Pilates, muscle relaxers, and a standing desk didn't fix your chronic neck and back pain, maybe this hunk of plastic will. You can't be sure until you spend $99.99 on it!

Vacations for Solo Travelers Ad: Try our boutique group adventures for solo travelers.
Translation: You've reached an age demographic where most of your friends have probably coupled up and it's getting harder to make new friends. We also noticed that you recently bought fine jewelry for yourself. Instead of sitting at home, draped in your new adornments, waiting for death, why not go on vacation with a bunch of strangers? You could end up in a beautiful location, surrounded by attractive eligible suitors vying for your attention—like an episode of *The Bachelor*! Or it could be a week-long blind date with no easy escape and unfortunate financial repercussions should you try to leave—also a bit like *The Bachelor*! Can you afford not to give it a try though?

Egg Freezing Cycle Ad: For just $5,000 per egg-freezing cycle, we can help you keep your options open for the future.
Translation: We noticed you clicked on both the fine jewelry ad and the vacations for solo travelers ad. This just felt like the next logical step.

CBT Ad: Learn cognitive behavioral therapy today and start feeling better tomorrow.

Translation: After a certain number of consecutive hours spent scrolling your seemingly endless feed, Instagram is morally and legally obligated to connect you with mental health resources to combat the effects of "compare and despair" culture. We, along with the US Surgeon General, highly recommend you seek help now. Or maybe just turn off your phone and interact with something that isn't constantly trying to monetize your every thought, feeling, and character trait.

Seven Signs It's Time for Face Creams

AS A WOMAN, IT CAN BE HARD TO KNOW WHEN IT'S THE right time to start coating your countenance in gelatinous globs of slippery face slime. For most of us, it's probably right around the time that our fertility, and therefore our value to society, begins to decline. Fortunately, if you're vigilant, there are several earlier indicators that can help you know when to start applying a slew of age-defying goops to your visage—thus prolonging your worth. Here are the signs to watch out for:

1. You just started to feel okay about yourself. If you've recently experienced a rise in self-esteem, increased self-assurance, or—God forbid—genuine confidence, it might be time to start slathering your face in goo every morning and night. This subtle indicator usually arises right around the time you start to shake off the painful uncertainty of your early twenties. You'll know it's happening when, for the first time since the onset of adolescence, you finally start to feel comfortable in your own skin; that is your cue to start worrying about said skin. Is it starting to sag a little under your neck? Is that a fine line under your eye, or a wrinkle? What exactly is the difference between the two? If you go to the internet for answers, you'll probably find various beauty publications saying that you should've been applying at least two face creams a night since your eighteenth birthday—the day that marks the beginning of a woman's descent into old cronehood. By beauty magazine standards you're already behind. It's a shame no one ever told you prevention is key, but you can still work with the quickly decaying canvas you've got.

2. Your acne is under control. This is a sign that it's time to move on to bigger and better skin conditions. You may have just won a long battle with the same acne that's plagued you since you were a teen or squelched your burgeoning hormonal acne—thanks to that fun second puberty thing no one likes to talk about—but either way, congratulations! The only downside to aging out of your acne is that it means you're definitely aging. It's probably time you traded in the salicylic acid of your youth for hyaluronic acid—the preferred face acid of decrepit old harpies. Don't worry, you're going to love drizzling plumping serums from medical droppers onto your rapidly maturing pimple-free cheeks. Let the sticky goo slide over that dried-out slab of beef jerky you call a complexion and lubricate it back to the youthful glow of your Clearasil days. Just cross your fingers that all the hydration doesn't trigger a breakout.

3. Your facial muscles are showing signs that you actually use them. If you've been making facial expressions all willy-nilly your whole life, it's absolutely time for several face creams and possibly an intervention. You're going to need multiple serums, day creams, night creams, eye creams, topical collagen, edible collagen, one of those vibrating laser scrubbers, and a huge attitude adjustment. Nature may have given you a truly wondrous range of intricate facial expressions to communicate with, but what are you trying to prove by using all of them? It's going to take a lot of expensive face goop to fill the deep grooves you've created with your wanton indulgence in things like smiles and laughter. Now is the time to crack down and limit the use of your overworked facial muscles. You may even want to consider rationing out exactly how many more times you can afford to make certain expressions before the lines become permanent. If you're an excessive user, you may already be down to just one frown a year. High-end face creams applied with a neutralizing jade roller should smooth out the worst of your facial kinks—and the calming crystal energy might help offset some of your more effusive emotional outbursts. However, if you don't stop emoting so frivolously, nothing will be able to slow your transformation into a weather-beaten ogress.

4. You've reached an age where you would've already been married and had two kids in the 1950s. Your grandmother started slathering on cold cream way before she got married and had your mother. And back then they got their face creams from the same companies that made napalm, so thank your lucky stars that all you have to deal with is questionably harvested snail mucus. Your grandma understood the youth-preserving benefits of a nightly cosmetic embalming. Without those chemicals she might not have been able to secure a husband and ensure your future existence. Seems like the least you could do is slap on a moisturizing night cream in her honor.

5. You've realized that the women in beauty commercials talking about fine lines and wrinkles are now your age. This one may be a little shocking at first. In your younger days, you probably thought of those women—the ones smiling against white backdrops and swiping globs of clear goo onto their invisible crow's-feet—as almost elderly. Welcome to the horrifying realization that they weren't even middle-aged. And guess what? Now they're talking to *you*. You're officially the target demographic for brightening, whitening, toning, and tightening. Up until age twenty-five, it's all Lash Blast-Off-Your-Face Mascara and Luxe Deluxe Doe-eyed Liner. But once you reach the hard age cutoff, all you get is revitalizing, repairing, elasticizing, collagen-boosting, retinol-injecting, silicon-slapping, bone-building, death-defying creams, creams, and more creams. The time for beauty products with fun colors and sparkles has passed—eyeshadow isn't going to keep you from looking like the twenty-six-year-old crypt keeper you are. It's all antioxidants and under eye creams from here on out, so listen to the nice ladies on TV promising you that eternal youth can be found in a series of tiny glass jars.

6. You willingly go to bed early. This is your body trying to tell you that it's ready for a ten-step skincare regimen. Not only do you need your beauty sleep, but you need time before bed to apply multiple layers of cream. When you're done, your face should feel like a cosmetic tiramisu or an untouched archeological dig site—there should be layers upon layers to dig through. Fun fact: Scientists have assumed for years that all dinosaurs were covered in scales because there's no sign that any of them ever applied face creams.

7. You have discretionary income. If you have slightly more money than you require for the bare minimum of subsistence living, then it is absolutely time for face creams. Forget about contributing more to your retirement fund; your face is the 401(k) of your body and it needs creams—extremely expensive creams. And let's be honest, if you've worked long enough in our capitalist society to have any kind of discretionary income, your visage must be haggard, exhausted, and in need of moisture. Fortunately, money is exactly the solution to this problem. Just find the most expensive creams and pick the ones that come in the smallest jars. The more you pay per ounce now, the less likely you are to be mistaken for a wicked old fairy-tale hag later. Although, if you want to embrace the wicked witch thing, you could always ditch the creams entirely and go for the tried and true "bathing in the blood of innocents" method—it's cost-effective, and you certainly wouldn't be the first. Anything to stay looking young, right ladies?

What You Need Is Some Very Expensive Underwear

THANK YOU FOR CHOOSING OUR LUXURY LINGERIE BOU-
tique for your upscale underwear needs. Try not to look so surprised that a brick-and-mortar store, which exists solely to cover
your private parts with decorative trappings, is able to stay in
business in this economy. Do you mind if I immediately measure
the parts of your body you're most self-conscious about? You
might think that you know your bra size, or that you don't want
me to invade your personal space with my measuring tape, but
trust me, you're wrong. Most women don't know their true bra
size, probably because their teeny tiny brains can barely grasp the
concept of measurement—or maybe because the bra measurement system is an unnecessarily complicated vestige leftover from
old garment construction practices. Either way, let's get you measured, then we can talk about what we can do to make this whole
saggy bag of flesh more appealing. Don't worry, there's nothing
that can't be saved with some exorbitantly expensive underwear.

First things first, what are the styles of your current under-
garments? I'm sorry, but 100 percent cotton is not a style. Do
you prefer to have your breasts shoved up from the bottom or
sort of squeezed from all directions? Would you like rigid wires
that stab the sensitive flesh just below your arms or structureless
triangles of lace that make your nipples itch? Can we interest

you in padding thick enough to qualify for most contact sports, or perhaps some completely transparent mesh that makes your bosom look like two coconuts trying to escape a fishing net? We also have a wide variety of both load-bearing and non-load-bearing straps, depending on how functional you'd like your new bra to be. It might seem counterintuitive, but the more functional ones cost less.

Since you aren't sure about brassieres just yet, why don't we start with some bottoms? We have some excellent styles that show zero panty lines and zero understanding of how most women's bodies are shaped. They're guaranteed to ride up your butt crack and sit there in an uncomfortable wad, but don't worry, you'll be the only one who knows they're there—unless of course you're caught attempting to dislodge them. Would you like to try on a pair in spandex, Lycra, nylon, or synthetic lace? I'll bring you all four since you're going to get a yeast infection no matter which non-breathable fabric you choose. Plus, you'll need to buy a few pairs if you want to decrease the odds that you'll be caught wearing those frightful full-coverage cotton contraptions the next time someone makes amorous advances toward you.

All right, I know I've already checked on your fitting room several times, but I'm getting a little concerned that none of these items are working for you. Why don't you show me your incredibly vulnerable body so that I can help you figure out how to arrange your genitals more attractively? See, now that I'm looking at you, I think I have just the thing. Have you ever tried shapewear? It would take everything you've got going on here, pack it into a spandex tube, and mold it into the shape of an hourglass—the only acceptable body type for a very sexy lady. Here, stop silently crying and have this glass of champagne while I go find you a waist trainer. You're going to love the way it makes you feel when you've worn it for too long and it starts to gently displace the organs in your abdominal cavity.

Okay, now that you've tried on most of what we have in the store, it's time to make some tough decisions. Do you want the tissue-thin white lace bralette that costs as much as thirty-five lattes, or the strapless black silk push-up bra that costs more than a pair of AirPods Pro? I think you should just get both. That means you'll also need to get both pairs of matching panties for about the same price as two tickets to Disney World. And don't forget that gorgeous shapewear bodysuit that you should probably never take off for as long as you live—it's totally worth the price of a short domestic roundtrip flight. Since you got a free glass of champagne in the process, it's practically like you had a coupon.

Trust me, I wouldn't be encouraging you this way if I didn't honestly think that you needed every single one of these garments in order to fit within the narrow constraints of what our culture deems conventionally attractive. But, in the end, this is all about you and what you need to feel good about yourself. Though, if you ask me—the person earning a commission and financially benefiting from this exchange of goods—I'd say that what you need to feel good is multiple sets of very expensive underwear.

Maslow's Hierarchy of Wants

EVERYONE ALWAYS TALKS ABOUT MASLOW'S HIERARCHY of Needs, but no one ever mentions his less popular sequel, Maslow's Hierarchy of Wants. That's perhaps due to the general perception that sequels are never as good as the original, or it could be because people don't actually need anything in this hierarchy. Not that that's ever stopped anyone from wanting anything—or everything—before.

Tier 1: Basically Justifiable Wants

These refer to a person's most easily justified wants, like buying a $15 salad for lunch every day instead of bringing your lunch to work, or calling an Uber when you could just wait for the train or bus. They usually represent an effort to keep the body in a state of homeostatic satisfaction by coming up with any excuse to answer small cravings or seek increased convenience. For example, subscribing to one of those fancy meal kit boxes so that you'll "cook more during the week," telling yourself it's okay to order takeout when you're too tired to cook, and then getting a bottle of wine to go with dinner just because Wednesday rhymes with rosé. Someone's basically justifiable wants must be met before they can move to the next tier of wanting. After all, if you really want to Postmates an Oreo McFlurry at 1 a.m., you're going to have to focus all your energy on justifying it.

Tier 2: Fun Wants

Once people's basically justifiable wants are met, the next desire that arises is for fun and frivolity. Our fun wants are apparent from the moment we come out of the womb demanding access to Diplo concerts, trampolines, and hard drugs. However, not everyone's fun wants are the same. They can range from simple things like having access to the most popular streaming services, to climbing up very large dangerous rocks and almost dying for the thrill of it. Other examples include: going to dance clubs that charge $20 for a vodka soda, doing a foot peel that removes a grossly satisfying amount of foot skin, doing a bunch of hallucinogenic mushrooms, or the act of buying any item you don't explicitly need (e.g., probiotic lip gloss, a decorative shark's jaw, a romantic prairie dress that looks nice on Instagram—but later reminds you that you're not always comfortable performing femininity in real life). It all counts as frivolous fun.

Tier 3: Social Wants

Next are people's social wants. It's not enough to have love, acceptance, and belonging in real life. People want to be socially connected to every single person they know, at all times, through at least three different morally dubious social media platforms. They want to be able to see what people they haven't talked to since high school are ordering for dinner at Maggiano's. They want to know about the extravagant two-week vacation to Europe their annoying coworker could somehow afford. They want to know if their friends went to a concert last night without them. They want to know the controversial political opinions of D-list celebrities and extended family members. And, most of all, they want to compare all of it to their own life. What they *don't* want is to feel like they've missed out on something. To avoid this feeling, people stay constantly connected, regardless of the effect it may have on their mental health.

Tier 4: Validation Wants

At the fourth tier is the desire for validation. When the wants at the bottom three levels have been satisfied, it becomes increasingly important to receive praise, attention, and approval from others. People want to have their efforts recognized for starting Instagram accounts with pictures of dogs that look like waffles. They want all their friends to know they're making a short film, to prove their personal worth. They want praise for that funny thing they said in the group text, and they want attention for every life milestone they reach. Most of them just want the approval of their parent(s) in literally any capacity. However, people who try to satisfy their validation wants by achieving success, praise, and recognition from others tend to feel content only temporarily. As a result, there is some academic speculation that a person's want for validation can never truly be fulfilled.

Tier 5: Want Actualization

Finally, at the very peak of the hierarchy we have want actualization. This concept hinges on the idea that what a person can want, they must want in order to achieve their full wanting potential as a human being. Want-actualizing people are want-aware, concerned with the growth of their wants, less concerned with the wants of others, and just generally want it all. Very few people have ever reached this highest tier, but those who have say that they still want more.

Have You Tried Love, Sex, or Some Combination of the Two?

ON LOVING DUKES, MONSTERS, AND
RECHARGEABLE ELECTRONICS.

Have You Tried a Duke?

MOST PEOPLE THINK IT'S DIFFICULT TO FIND LOVE, that it requires luck, hard work, and endless hours spent swiping through dating apps. But I fall in love about five times a day. I fall in love with people reading books on the train, famous actors getting profiled by the *New York Times*, construction workers holding stop signs in front of road work zones, and every reasonably amusing stand-up comedian I've ever seen. Just the other day I fell madly in love with a runner who passed me on the street. I pictured not only our whirlwind romance, but also the successful bed-and-breakfast we'd open in Vermont once we wed.

The key to falling in love like this is not minding that it's all a bit one-sided. Because it's much easier to be in love with the idea of a person than it is to be in love with an actual person who has strong opinions about modern art, refuses to eat seafood, and insists on always occupying the right side of the bed.

Lately, I haven't been limiting my amorous imaginings to mere living, breathing human beings. As easy as it is to fall in love with real people whose lives you create for yourself in your head, it's even easier to fall in love with fictional people some other person has created for you—often with the express purpose of wish fulfillment in mind. That's why I've once again started reading romance novels.

To my great surprise and delight, romance books have been a soothing balm for the immense sense of dissatisfaction that sometimes creeps up on me at night when I'm alone in my apartment. It's a strange lack of fulfillment, which I sometimes confuse for a very strong sugar craving. It mostly happens when I've been on my own for too long, and it likes to strike at inconvenient times, like when everyone I know is asleep. Fortunately, fictional people are more readily available at odd hours of the night than real people. So, when panic starts to settle into the vulnerable, empty places of my soul, I can quickly stem the flow with a titillating story about some lady in a ballgown who might be utterly ruined for touching a man's pinky finger in public. It's been a truly wonderful coping mechanism.

My interest in the romance genre was initially rekindled by *Outlander*, a television show based on a series of novels about an English World War II battlefield nurse who accidentally time travels through a set of extremely phallic magic rocks and ends up smooching an impossibly perfect eighteenth-century Scottish man. It's like a Russian nesting doll of romantic period dramas. After finishing the show, the books became my gateway into romance.

It wasn't long after reading *Outlander* that I started to amass a drawer full of books with varying degrees of Scotland-related puns on the covers—titles like *A Scot in the Dark*, *A Scot Ties the Knot*, and *Some Like It Scot*. Because, as it turns out, romance books these days are charmingly self-aware. Which makes it even more disappointing that there's still so much unfair stigma attached to reading them—so much that I used to be too embarrassed to display my depraved drawer of shirtless, sword-wielding Scottish men on my bookshelf.

There's this ridiculously outdated notion that the romance genre is for silly women who are too weak-minded for real literature, but this couldn't be further from the truth. In fact, a study I can't remember the name of right now found that most romance readers have, at minimum, a bachelor's degree. Not to mention that a substantial number of popular romance writers have gone to Ivy League schools and held, or continue to hold, high-powered jobs. For example, successful romance author Courtney Milan got a law degree and clerked for Supreme Court Justices Sandra Day O'Connor and Anthony M. Kennedy before writing her first book. And, before she ran for governor of Georgia and turned Georgia blue for Joe Biden in the 2020 presidential election, Stacey Abrams wrote romance thrillers.

It would seem to me that the stigma surrounding romance novels is just another case of people deciding that something is less valuable because it is, in most instances, made by women for other women. Not to mention that the popularity of these books dares to imply that women might actually be interested in sex. In fact, many of them—especially the more modern ones—create whole worlds where women take control of their sexual pleasure and, God forbid, get what they want. What could be more scandalous in a society founded by a bunch of patriarchal, sex-negative puritans?

Thankfully, I've gotten over both my single-minded fascination with men in woolen skirts and my societally ingrained shame about reading romance—which is good because I was running out of space in the drawer. I've since ventured into the wider subgenre of historical romance to fill the empty spaces in my soul. But as I started to branch out from my preferred archetype of "big Scottish dude with big Scottish sword," I couldn't help but notice some of the other consistently recurring heroes on the shelves. There's the knight in shining armor, the pirate with a heart of gold, the rake in need of reform, a shocking number of gambling den owners, and a respectable sprinkling of earls, viscounts, and marquesses, but none is so prominent as *the duke*. There are more dukes in the romance aisles of libraries and bookstores than you can shake a jewel-encrusted scepter at. There are so many that I started collecting them like trading cards. Because it wasn't uncomfortable enough to be the only person at the indie bookstore in Brooklyn checking out the kissing books instead of the feminist literature display; I also had to be the person taking pictures of the sex books "for personal research." I'm sure it looked very normal and well-adjusted.

However, it was worth it, because I now have a whole folder of images on my phone called "dukes," and for a time this folder was my favorite ice breaker at social events. I would wait for an awkward silence or a lull in conversation and then I'd just blurt out, "Would you like to see my dukes?" with all the manic energy of an eccentric anthropologist who thinks they've found the missing link. Because again, I am very normal and well-adjusted.

The duke phenomenon, however, is not news to those in the know. It's a widely recognized and acknowledged trope in the romance-reading community. But, as a relative newcomer, it felt like a shocking discovery I needed to share with anyone who would listen. "Ladies love dukes!" I would exclaim to the unlucky person sitting next to me at a wedding reception. "What do you think the sexiest royal title is?" I would ask new acquaintances at parties. I was completely fascinated, and I wanted an explanation for the phenomenon. Trust me, if you saw all the dukes together in one image folder, you'd want an explanation too.

I have personally come across fifty-eight dukes in the wild—*Romancing the Duke, No Good Duke Goes Unpunished, A Duke by Default, The Duke Who Didn't, How to Love a Duke in Ten Days*, just to name a few. And that's only counting the ones with the word "duke" somewhere in the title. There are many more that feature a duke but don't advertise it on the cover. To determine the true number of dukes in romance, I'd have to do far more research.

Despite my incomplete data, I do have a completely unscientific, entirely speculative hypothesis for why dukes are so popular. There is something the dukes have that other romance heroes do not, and that's the exact right combination of power and responsibility. Kings and gambling den owners are powerful, but they have countries and businesses to run—they can't just spend the afternoon in bed, rubbing your feet and helping you plot revenge on the mean ladies who laughed at your unfashionable reticule at the ball last week. Dukes, however, *do* have time for that kind of thing, and without sacrificing much in the way of power. They have status, but they're also at their leisure to take you for a spin in the park with their fancy new team of horses, or to sit patiently while you're fitted for a new hat covered in the trendiest taxidermy birds.

In romance books, the duke always makes his love interest his number one priority. He uses all his power and lofty status to take care of that person—even when he's supposed to be a rakish bad boy duke with a scandalous reputation, or an emotionally traumatized recluse duke with disfiguring facial scars. Dukes just can't help themselves. They might talk a big game about being free-spirited, debauched, or uninterested, but if you're their person:

- They make sure you're comfortable.
- They make sure you're well-fed.
- They have baths drawn for you in impressive copper tubs.
- They outfit you with only the finest silks and linens for your wardrobe, despite your protests of "Oh, I couldn't possibly" and "This burlap sack I'm wearing is fine."

- They murder your enemies for you if the occasion calls for it.

- And, even though most of these books take place before the twentieth century, their position on sex is firmly "You come first."

Considering all this, why wouldn't you want a duke? As someone who was born tired, I would like nothing more than to have a handsome, intelligent member of the aristocracy cater to my every need and whim. I feel like I'm not supposed to admit that because it doesn't really go with the "I'm a strong independent person" narrative I usually try to spin for myself, but even the strongest, most independent people need a break sometimes.

When you look past all the horses and corsets, what most duke books do is let you imagine a world where someone with unlimited time and resources wants to fully devote themselves to loving and supporting you. In our modern, fast-paced, productivity-obsessed culture, it's not surprising that this would be a popular fantasy. Who needs self-care when you have duke-care? Let the duke clean up after dinner tonight. Let the duke file your taxes this year. Let the duke explain why you can't make it to that social engagement you've been trying to get out of all week. Let the duke make life safe and easy and full of unconditional love, which occasionally manifests itself as mutually gratifying sex in the back of a carriage.

Personally, I've found that romance books are an excellent coping mechanism for my nondescript feelings of longing and loneliness, whether they involve a duke or not. Because all romances have one thing in common regardless of subgenre. No matter if the book is about a devilish reputation-ruining duke, or an emotionally intelligent nonbinary alien, it's going to have a happy ending. It's a requirement of the genre as a whole. And nothing soothes my anxiety like being able to start a love story knowing that no matter what happens, things are going to work out in the end.

Admittedly, neither my habit of falling in love with strangers nor my romance-reading habit completely satisfy my vague sugar-like cravings for reciprocated human intimacy. But whether you're imagining running off to Berlin with the cashier at Trader Joe's, or reading about a fictional aristocrat who wants to do hand stuff at the opera, it's fun to lose yourself in a little romantic escapism. Just remember to come back to the real world every once in a while. After all, you wouldn't want to miss your chance to meet an actual living, breathing person who can fill the aching gaps in your tortured soul—and annoy you with their opinions about modern art, their refusal to eat seafood, and their insistence on occupying the right side of the bed.

Romance Novel Summaries
for Real-Life Relationships

WOULD LIFE BE SEXIER IF OUR RELATIONSHIPS WERE written like the back cover of a mass market romance novel? Check out some of these bestselling titles to find out:

What She Really Wants for Dinner

Free-spirited culinary enthusiast Tim has big dreams about what's for dinner tonight. Maybe a *NYT Cooking* recipe that says it takes thirty minutes but actually takes two hours. Or maybe he'll do something with those frozen salmon fillets he got on sale at Whole Foods—the possibilities are endless! At least, that's what he thought before Erica came home from work and turned his kitchen upside down. Now, after several red-hot rounds of culinary rejection, temperatures are rising—and it's not just the preheating oven. Why can't Erica see that all he's ever wanted to do is give her the world on a seafood platter?

Strong-willed Erica knows exactly what she wants in life, but not what she wants for dinner. All she knows is that it's not whatever Tim is making tonight. How will she find the courage to tell the man she loves that he always overcooks the salmon? It's a dark secret that's been eating away at their relationship for months. Now, she's faced with an even bigger dilemma: She must somehow admit that what she really wants is someone else's cooking. How will he take it when she suggests bringing in outside food? Will he follow her into the hedonistic realm of delivery orders, or will he judge her for her illicit weeknight desires? His answer could change the fate of their relationship for . . . tonight, at the very least. Maybe even into tomorrow morning.

Will she let their love go hungry, or will she reveal . . . *What She Really Wants for Dinner.*

The Forbidden Question

Doomed to a life of romantic uncertainty, loving but sensitive Tiffany finds herself in an emotional stalemate she can't escape. After what she thought was a successful brunch outing with her friends and new girlfriend, she can't help but notice that her beloved, Heather, has suddenly become silent and moody. Was it something she said at brunch? Something she did? A face she made? A breath she breathed? Is this the silent conflict that will bring their relationship crashing down around them? She has so many questions, and yet she's afraid to know the answers. The pressure is almost unbearable, but she must find the courage to ask the most illicit question of all: Are you mad at me?

Introverted Heather is the very definition of the strong silent type. Enamored with kind and caring Tiffany, there is only one thing in life she loves as much as her new girlfriend, and that's being alone. That morning's brunch had its moments, but ultimately required more small talk than her limited powers of conversation could muster. If she had to ask one more of Tiffany's peripheral acquaintances what they did last weekend, while feigning genuine interest, she was going to crush her bottomless mimosa glass in her fist. Home at last, all she wants is a little peace and quiet. What she gets is a crisis of faith from her partner that shakes her to her very irritated core. Utterly devoted, Heather would do anything to make Tiffany happy—anything that is, but answer that dreaded question.

Soon, they'll put their love, and interpersonal communication skills, to the test. Because no relationship can escape . . . *The Forbidden Question.*

The Screens Between Us

When fiery redhead Liz first meets happy-go-lucky Jeremy, she can't help but fall for the way he looks into her eyes and actually listens when she speaks. She knows he's the one the moment he reveals he has a healthy relationship with his mother. However, when their instant attraction causes them to immediately fall into bed together, she makes a shocking discovery. Nothing could've prepared her for the raw passion, the fire, and the frequency with which Jeremy looks at his phone. Instead of gazing lovingly into her eyes as they lay in bed together, he gazes adoringly at sports stats, the front page of Reddit, and the unending scroll of TikTok. Will Liz retreat into a screen of her own, or will she fight to keep the attention of the man she loves?

Carefree and charming Jeremy has met his match in feisty no-nonsense Liz. Sure, she does look a bit like his mom with that flaming red hair, but not in a weird way—not really. From the second they locked eyes, he's been determined to make her his forever, or at least until three years from now when they're both kind of bored with each other and ready to move on. No power on Earth could convince him to relinquish her until then, except perhaps one—the power of the phone. Compulsive scrolling is just a part of Jeremy's nature that he thinks Liz should learn to accept. But when she refuses to compete with a machine, a battle of wills ensues that promises to break both hearts and screens.

Will love conquer all? Or will they be torn apart by . . . *The Screens Between Us?*

Mistletoe or Mezcal?

Hardworking and intrepid Alex wants nothing more than to plan a tropical vacation getaway for the holidays this year. Tantalizing dreams of mezcal margaritas and banana daiquiris dance in his head as he imagines himself and his boyfriend, David, getting tan on a beach in Tulum. Unfortunately, all David can talk about is going home to see his family in snowy Chicago. Nothing could be further from Alex's vision of spending Christmas in a Speedo than sitting at a table in suburban Illinois, listening to David's uncle call himself a fiscal conservative, while slurping down spoonfuls of marshmallow ambrosia salad. He'll have to use all his powers of seduction to convince David that they should be renewing their love somewhere warm, not letting it wither in a city cold enough to rival the North Pole.

Lovable methodical David can't wait to go home for the holidays, like he does every year. He knows wild, adventurous Alex would rather take a steamy tropical vacation, but what's Christmastime without snow and at least one uncomfortable conversation with your family about politics? He knows that with enough time, he can win Alex over and into his twin-size childhood bunk beds. The only thing he's up against is the ticking clock. Will he be able to make Alex see things his way before the price of flights to Chicago start to skyrocket? Or are they destined to have a decidedly unhappy holiday?

Only time will tell if this holiday will bring . . . *Mistletoe or Mezcal.*

Romancing the Phone

Successful and always put together, Emily has it all: a job that pays a living wage, an apartment that has at least one window in each room, and friends that bail on their plans to hang out only 30 percent of the time. There's just one thing keeping her from achieving each and every goal on her five-year-plan checklist: finding a stable romantic partner. Despite the fact that she's active on every dating app available, all she's got to show for it is enough unsolicited dick pics to complete a successful double-blind study of men's genital health in her area. That is, until she comes across Sam's somewhat dull but red-flag-free profile.

When down-on-his-luck Sam matched with the lovely Emily, he knew this was his chance to turn things around for himself. He's matched with plenty of other women before, but he's never made it past the initial texting phase with any of them. Some person-alities just don't translate well digitally, and Sam's is one of them. With straightforward, goal-oriented Emily, he feels like this might just be the time he finally gets past the awkward "Hi, what's up?" part of the conversation. In fact, he's already fantasizing about moving on to more intimate topics with her—like whether that's her dog in her profile photo. His most fervent desire is to simply hold her interest long enough to invite her on an in-person date. However, he'll have to control his wild conversational urges—he doesn't want to scare her off before he can fan their slow burn small talk into a texting inferno.

Love is complicated face to face, and it's even harder when you're stuck . . . *Romancing the Phone*.

Six Upsettingly Realistic Sex Toys Nobody Asked For

AT TOO REAL TOYS INC., WE ARE COMMITTED TO BRINGing you the most lifelike sexual experiences a person can have with a piece of technologically enhanced silicone. Our high-quality, body-safe products are so realistic, you might not even know the difference between our toys and the real thing. Here are the newest items to hit our growing product lineup:

The Not-So-Dirty Talker

A palm-sized, external vibe that's perfect for beginners. In addition to its five vibration settings, it also has five conversational settings, specifically designed for those who like to get to know the object of their lust. On its first setting, it can tell you its full name, occupation, and place of birth, but crank it up to five and get ready to hear about its complex relationship with its overbearing mother and emotionally distant father.

The Edger Pro

This sleek, internal vibrator has ten speeds that will have you climaxing all night long, and ten patented blanket-hogging patterns that will rip the covers off you all night long—just like a real bedmate! Set it to sleep mode and get ready to feel it slowly spin, winding itself in the blankets and nudging you to one side of the bed. It won't quit until it has you teetering on the very edge, curled into a position that would give your chiropractor heart palpitations. We promise the Edger Pro will never leave you hanging; it'll push you over the edge in every way possible.

The Phantom

It may look like a basic silicone dildo, but the Phantom is one of the most high-tech, single-use products on the market. After just one amazing night of bliss, the Phantom activates its special one-of-a-kind ghosting mechanism, allowing it to quietly disappear the moment you doze off. We guarantee you won't find a single trace of it when you wake up, not even the receipt from its purchase.

The Jerk

If you prefer a dildo that's going to stick around for more than one romp, we highly recommend the Jerk. It's both dependable and exciting, because anytime you use it vaginally, there's a 50 percent chance that it'll "accidentally" veer off course toward your butt. The special automatic jerking maneuver happens suddenly and without warning (or lube), but it always stops the moment you shriek, "Not that hole!" Note: If you start out using the Jerk anally, it will do the exact same thing except in reverse, until you yell, "Oh my God, how many times do I have to explain UTIs and the delicate balance of vaginal bacteria to you?!"

The Josh

This is our answer to the RealDoll, but with even more lifelike details. Right now, we're only offering one standard biologically male body type, but you can choose the color of his eyes, his hair, and his Carhartt beanie. Josh has all the features you could ever want in an anatomically male sex doll, but with added elements that take the experience to a whole new level of realism. For example, you can remove all of Josh's clothes, except for his socks—those stay on even when you're getting intimate. Josh doesn't make emotive sexual noises, but he does automatically emit loud snoring sound effects less than ten seconds after climax. This feature cannot be deactivated and lasts up to eight hours! Also, one of Josh's hands is permanently posed with his fingers in the "Shocker" position—he's such a funny guy.

The Womb-light

The Womb-light is our first penetrative toy designed for a penis. It looks like a typical Fleshlight to the untrained eye, but our model has an exclusive feature you won't find anywhere else: the Womb-light can become pregnant! That's right, if you have unprotected sex with this toy, it will conceive, gestate, and give birth to a real human baby, which you will be legally and financially responsible for until it comes of age—hot! It's unquestionably our most true-to-life sex toy yet.

Dear Mother and Father, My Monster Boyfriend Is Coming to Dinner

DEAR MOTHER AND FATHER,

I'm writing to inform you that my monster boyfriend is coming to dinner. Don't worry, he's nothing like the last boyfriend I brought home. In fact, he's like no one I've ever met before. I think you're really going to like him, and I can't wait for you to see how crazy we are about each other. Like, honestly, I don't think I could leave him if I tried. I just want to mention a few minor things before we come over, but I promise there's absolutely no reason to be alarmed.

First off, he has claws. I know! You always taught me that bad hygiene is a sign of bad character, but it's really not his fault. No matter how short we cut the pesky things in the morning, they just grow back—three inches long and razor sharp—by bedtime. He's learning to be very gentle with them though. It's been so long since he's used them to slash apart the furniture, or old portraits of himself (they were painted before the curse and he feels like they're mocking him sometimes). Plus, they come in handy when he's fighting off the bloodthirsty beasts that surround his enchanted property. They've attempted to eat me several times for trying to leave the premises. If he didn't have his own set of fangs and claws, I don't know if we'd be able to come visit you at all!

You're going to notice a large sexy scar on his face. Whatever you do, don't stare at it, don't ask about it, and don't point out how perfectly placed it is in relation to his facial features. I find it dangerously appealing rather than disfiguring, but he's still very sensitive about it.

He can be a bit moody. Due to his fragile, brooding nature, he is occasionally subject to fits of temper. These emotional eruptions are usually harmless and mostly end with a bit of property damage and a bellowed order to join him for dinner—it shouldn't be a problem this weekend since we'll be having dinner already. Rest assured that, to my knowledge, there have never been any human casualties as a result of these outbursts, though they can be very hard on the drywall and any nearby livestock. Just the other night, I tried to suggest that there are better ways to get to know people than imprisoning them in your enchanted castle, and he was so upset that he burst through the library wall, tore across the grounds, and absconded with some of our neighbor's cattle. That reminds me, you might want to order an extra steak or seven for Sunday—no need to cook them!

You might not notice it at first, but he is a few hundred years older than me. Fortunately, the curse keeps him physically frozen in time, so it's only a May–December relationship psychologically— and age is just a number anyway, right? Eighteenth century? Twenty-first century? They're practically neighboring centuries. Plus, you've always said I'm mature for my age.

He has this funny quirk that he only ever wears black. I'm not sure if it's because it's slimming or foreboding, but he's very fond of dark colors. He also hasn't updated his look much since the eighteenth century, so capes and long flowing robes are still a staple of his wardrobe. So far, I've managed to talk him into replacing some of his tailored waistcoats with a cashmere sweater or two. The next step is convincing him to trim his long dark hair, so it stops mysteriously obscuring his face in a way that frightens people. Once that's been handled, I can start weaning him off the capes and robes. Right now, he's very attached to storming in and out of rooms with a blast of icy wind and a sweep of his tattered black cloak. I'm sure you'll get to witness this firsthand when he makes his entrance at dinner. You'll know it's about to happen when the room fills with a strange otherworldly fog and a red-eyed raven lands on the china cabinet. Just ignore the bird's piercing cries; it knows it's not supposed to beg for table scraps.

Sometimes he has wings—not the feathery angel kind, but big, leathery bat wings. Don't think about it too hard. I've made him promise not to take them out at dinner.

He prefers to communicate telepathically. His large fangs and deep growling voice make it hard to verbalize, so he might invade your mind and speak to you that way. It may feel weird at first, having him in there, but I promise he won't implant any fake memories or bend you to his will. Whatever happens, though, don't struggle. It significantly increases the odds that he'll accidentally break your mind and turn you into a drooling, brainless husk of your former self.

The last thing is that he doesn't technically need to eat food. I understand how that could be a bit confusing since we're all going to be sharing a meal together. He just has some very specific nutritional requirements that can't be met by strictly human fare. Of course, he loves eating raw meat for pleasure, but to regenerate his magic powers he needs fresh blood. Now, before you freak out, don't worry, he doesn't feed on me. He just really *really* wants to and thinks about it every second of every day. I see it as a beautiful test of his love. He cares about me so much that he's given his word that he'll never purposely slaughter me, drain the blood from my body, and feast upon my flesh. All I must do is make sure I never accidentally injure myself and bleed in his presence—not even a tiny paper cut. Also, once a month I must drive several hundred miles away to menstruate in a heavily guarded lockdown bunker. Every relationship has its compromises!

Now, I know you're probably thinking, "This man sounds like an absolute monster," and you wouldn't be totally wrong. He is indeed cursed to walk this earth in a profane beastly form, until such time as the spell can be lifted, but there's so much more to him than that. When we come to dinner this weekend, I want you to try to see what I see—a deeply misunderstood creature in need of love. Even though he struggles with communicating effectively, expressing love and affection, and understanding the impact of his power over others, I'm certain that, with a little time and immense effort, I can fix him. Honestly, aside from the curse and the castle and the wings, he's not really that different from most of the human men I've dated.

Mother and Father, I'm asking you to give him a chance. He might be a literal monster, but for reasons I'd rather not examine too closely with you, I find that incredibly hot. So, start doing whatever you need to do to get ready for this weekend, because like it or not, my monster boyfriend is coming to dinner!

Have You Tried Nature?

ON HIKING, MOUNTAINS, AND THE
BENEFITS OF NIGHTMARE SHACKS.

Have You Tried Walking around Outside for Fun?

I DIDN'T UNDERSTAND THE CONCEPT OF HIKING UNTIL fairly recently. I knew that it was something people enjoyed, and that it seemed to require special footwear, a Swiss Army knife, and some kind of pointlessly gendered childhood scout training. However, I didn't fully grasp why people found it fun or relaxing. I think this had a lot to do with the way I'd experienced nature for most of my life. I didn't have an aversion to it, but I didn't exactly equate it with relaxation either. Until my mid-twenties, this is what I knew to be true about the outdoors:

Nature is going to kill us all (and we probably deserve it)

I don't know what they teach in the US in second grade, but growing up in Canada, I learned about global warming. Right alongside the lesson on the water cycle and the wonders of the rain forest, they give the lesson on the impending environmental apocalypse. One of the first things I ever officially learned about nature was that it was potentially going to kill me. This wasn't how the teachers framed it, but it's certainly what I extrapolated from the information provided.

Climate change became my greatest fear, apart from spiders and the unspeakably disturbing clown in *The Brave Little Toaster* (look it up if you don't want to sleep tonight). What upset me most, though, was how calm my fellow classmates were about it. We had just been told that adults were mowing down forests, melting polar ice caps, and turning the world into a rapidly heating oven from which there was no escape. Why was no one else panicking? In an earnest attempt to do something about the situation, I began refusing to play with Pokémon cards, which my friends were obsessed with at the time. I was absolutely certain that the cards had been made from brutally murdered rain forest trees and I pitched my theory to anyone who would listen. This did not make me popular during recess.

As introductions to nature go, I'd say this one was relatively traumatic. In fact, it set off a cascade of fears about other possible natural disasters. When my family moved to Georgia, I became obsessed with Tornado Alley. When we moved to North Carolina, it was hurricanes and floods. For most of my early life, I viewed nature through the lens of looming environmental catastrophe. I was all but sure that it was trying to kill me, so it's not surprising that I didn't immediately see it as a place to kick back and relax.

Animals could kill us all if they really wanted to

From about third grade to middle school, my favorite television channel was Animal Planet. I watched almost every show that aired: *The Jeff Corwin Experience, Emergency Vets, Meerkat Manor,* and above all, *The Crocodile Hunter.* I adored Steve Irwin, despite the fact that he was consistently providing me with nature-based nightmare fuel. From spiders that dissolved human skin with one bite, to cobras that spit venom across great distances, and crocodiles that executed a move called "the death roll," Steve poked, wrestled, and released them all. As entertaining and educational as it was, it also gave me a visceral understanding of how animals might one day poison me, drown me, suffocate me, or rip me limb from limb. I developed a healthy respect for wildlife, but perhaps an overinflated sense of how likely I was to step on a copperhead every time I walked out my front door.

Outside is for manual labor

During my college summers in North Carolina, I worked as a crop scout for a local crop consultant. For those who did not go to school next to a cow pasture, a crop consultant is a person who scouts crops for farmers and collects data about weeds, pests, diseases, etc. They then make recommendations on how to treat the crops for those issues. I was the crop consultant's bug-counting, cotton-measuring, weed-identifying field minion. I worked eight to twelve hours a day, and I walked for most of that time. I walked through peanuts, squash, peppers, watermelons, wheat, asparagus, soybeans, and sweet potatoes, but mostly I walked through miles and miles of tobacco and cotton.

As I trudged through seven-foot-tall rows of flue-cured tobacco in 99 percent humidity and 99-degree heat, it never occurred to me that people might like to walk around and look at plants for fun. Walking around outside was my job. It was better than a desk job, but it was unquestionably work. Why would anyone stomp around in the woods for fun?

Taking all this into consideration, it shouldn't be hard to see why the concept of hiking didn't immediately click with me. It wasn't until I moved to New York City and spent a few months living directly on top of eight million other people that I thought, "Oh, this is why people like the woods." I'd never lived in a big city before and, while having my nightly homesick crying sessions on my apartment's unfinished roof, I had this overwhelming sensation of being stranded in an endless sea of humanity. Whereas before I had taken nature for granted, now every plant sprouting next to the sidewalk was a gift. Every blade of grass was suddenly a rare treat. My roommate and I would go to Prospect Park to see trees the way people go to the zoo to see exotic animals.

After my first summer of city living, I was invited to go on a casual fall hike in Bear Mountain State Park. By that time, I was more than ready to risk death by flash flood or copperhead bite if it meant getting to a place where there were more trees than people. Having never technically been on a hike before, I was a bit nervous. In my apprehension, I prepared for the day's outing as if it were a backcountry expedition. Would running shoes work on treacherous mountain slopes? Should I bring an extra pair of socks in case my feet got wet and frostbite set in? How much water was enough water? Would I have to rip off my inappropriate footwear and toss it into a gorge like Reese Witherspoon in *Wild*? It wasn't until we arrived at the trailhead that I came to my senses. This was just walking around outside—no different from crop scouting. This might even be safer than walking around a tobacco field because there was no chance of being chased by a wild boar or a farmer's loose hunting dogs. It was going to be fine. The better question was: Would it be fun?

Hauling a human body up an incline against the force of gravity is not, in and of itself, a fun activity. I would, however, describe the cumulative act of hiking as fun—the fresh air, the trees, the nice views, the way your body momentarily uncurls from its screen-accommodating pretzel posture. My first hike was gratifying in a way that felt completely natural. Maybe because, deep down, I instinctively knew that I was better suited to roaming the woods looking for edible plants and squirrels than roaming around lower Manhattan looking for a smoothie cart and a Sweetgreen. I didn't get frostbite, I wasn't forced to throw my shoes into a gorge, and for the first time I understood why people thought walking around outside was a hobby. In fact, it became one of my hobbies.

It wasn't long after my first hike that I started seeing trend pieces online coming to similar conclusions about the value of the outdoors. Though they used catchier terms like "forest bathing" and "nature therapy" to make their assertions, they were usually about this idea that spending time outside was healing for the mind and body. For me, this seemed to check out. I'd felt more relaxed after spending a day in the woods. Even just knowing that it was possible to get on a train and be out in nature in a matter of hours significantly reduced the number of times per week I was haunting my apartment rooftop, stress-crying like a melodramatic neighborhood ghost. I wanted to believe that spending time in the woods had the power to ease my anxiety and depression, and pop science seemed to agree with me.

As a result, I often fantasized about leaving civilization behind and escaping to the wilderness, where I'd become a full-time Lady of the Forest. In this fantasy, I'd be happy, despite my isolation and lack of access to personal hygiene products, living stress-free as a brooding woodland harpy. Ideally, I'd be incorporated into local folklore and used to scare naughty children into behaving—"Kayden, if you don't do your homework, the burned-out millennial forest witch is going to come for you!"

My extreme fantasy version of outdoor living probably wouldn't appeal to most people, but I know I'm not the only one who dreams of escaping civilization. There's been a notable cultural yearning to find peace and healing in nature over the last few years. It just tends to manifest itself in a friendlier, more Instagrammable format than "becoming a lady of the forest." For example:

The Tiny Home People—They're always posting escapist photos of their pint-sized A-frames perched on some scenic outlook, but they're one Pendleton blanket and a few strategically placed string lights away from being full-on People of the Forest.

The Thru-Hikers—There are loads of people who dream about doing long-distance hikes like the Appalachian Trail. The ones who follow through with it become Temporary People of the Forest.

The Foragers—These are the people who wake up one day and decide they want to forage for wild mushrooms or take classes in urban beekeeping. They're not totally committed to living in the forest yet, but they're well on their way.

The Van People—Let's not forget the #vanlifers, even though they can only be part-time People of the Forest because they need a variety of travel content (not just forest content) to appease the brands that sponsor their lifestyle.

There are also those who'd prefer not to live in a van or raise a horde of stinging insects on their roof, but instead fill their homes to the brim with houseplants. This is one of the more reasonable ways people manifest the desire to incorporate the stress-relieving properties of nature into their everyday lives. Though it has its own extremes. When houseplant people go overboard, they quickly go from "I just love having green things in the house" to "I live in a greenhouse now." I've seen apartments that look more like tiny jungles than human residences.

I'm happy to say I'm no longer confused as to why people find nature relaxing. Whether it's by surrounding themselves with houseplants or hiking a continuous three-thousand-mile trail through the wilderness, I get it now. My only issue is that I still sometimes feel like I'll never reap the full benefits of "nature therapy" unless I do something truly extreme. Small doses of the great outdoors couldn't possibly be enough to fix all my problems, right? In my head, it's not enough to just go for a walk or go camping. To fix everything, I'd need to make a huge change, like running off to live amongst the wolves or joining a commune upstate. The reality of those situations, however, is that I'd probably just end up with a different set of problems—like getting eaten by wolves or brainwashed by a cult.

It's taken some time to let go of my *Into the Wild*–style fantasies, but I'm finally realizing that fleeing to the forest to become some variety of hermit isn't going to solve everything. It's just a very dramatic way of running from my problems. If I'm going to be practical about solving my general state of stress and unhappiness, I need to accept that spending more time outdoors is just one part of learning to calm the fuck down. And—no matter how little time I get to spend walking around outside these days—some exposure to nature is always better than none.

I'm Moving to the Woods to Live in a Nightmare Shack

I AM CURRENTLY RENTING A SHOEBOX-SIZED APARTMENT with three roommates and no guarantee that there aren't rats throwing a rave inside the walls every night. It takes at least forty minutes to get anywhere using the subway, which requires me to cram myself into a metal tube with hundreds of other people—essentially forming a speeding underground city sausage. I then arrive at work, where they expect me to spend 90 percent of my brief time on this earth listening to people say words like "synergy" and "micro-influencer" without visibly cringing. I must also tolerate them referring to my time as "bandwidth," as if I'm some kind of algorithmically optimized computing unit, programmed to spit out content for them. If I'm lucky, I might go home and match with someone on a dating app who sends me an unsolicited picture of their genitals taken from an unflattering angle. In light of the cumulative stress of these situations, I've made the only logical decision available to me: I'm moving to the woods to live in a nightmare shack.

I've been searching real estate websites for weeks now to see what I can afford, and I was shocked to find that the mortgage payment for a delightful little shack of horrors upstate is less than my current monthly rent. There are some lovely options once you start getting into areas that aren't accessible by emergency services, and you wouldn't believe the space! The place I'm looking at right now has 1,500 square feet of dirt floors and not a single sheet of drywall, but that will just make it all the easier to commune with nature. There won't be a single thing between my body and the forest floor—and everything that lives on the forest floor. Why rush to insulate the walls and lay down a foundation?

Plus, I'll have time to learn all kinds of handy skills once I move out to the woods and leave my soulless city job behind. I can see myself now, hiking into a sleepy little town each morning, making an honest living as a part-time shopkeeper, an occasional craft fair vendor, or a quirky seasonal cafe owner. Movies and TV shows about people who leave the city behind have led me to believe that these charming noncommittal occupations are readily available in all small towns, and that they provide enough income to pay for extensive home repairs. I'll need to install some kind of heat source in my shack by winter!

Saving money will be easier once I partially withdraw from society to live out amongst the trees. Sure, I'll have to invest in some repairs to my shack, like digging a well so I can have running water and exterminating the family of poltergeists living in the attic (local legend says they've been there since 1752), but at least I won't be tempted to waste money on oat milk lattes and avocado toast anymore. Did you know those two things alone are the main reason why my generation can't afford to buy homes or save for retirement? Not me though! I'm dropping out of the rat race and shacking up in the woods.

At first, I thought that giving up on city life might be tough, but who needs to live near bars and restaurants when you could live within walking distance of an old, abandoned quarry, a haunted mining shaft, and scores of hungry bears? Plus, there's so much to do around the shack. It needs to be painted, reshingled, demolished, exorcised, and rebuilt from the ground up. All those little projects are what make a shack in the woods a home. If you're thinking, "Won't you get lonely?" don't worry, I'll have the creatures of the forest to keep me company. Who needs a family when you have a family of possums living under the heap of dilapidated wood where your porch used to be?

That's not to say I won't interact with people anymore—I'm only planning on being semi-reclusive. All my friends will be more than welcome to escape the bustle of city life and visit me out in the woods. The shack has plenty of space for guests, but depending on the time of year—and the activities of forest predators—we may just want to huddle together in one room for the majority of the time. It'll bring us closer together, and closer to a more natural state of being—one that doesn't include bathing regularly or becoming a cog in the capitalist machine. Because human beings weren't meant to live in towering stacks of concrete, pressed together like high-tech sardines. We weren't meant to ruin our eyesight and cervical spines, staring into glowing screens for twelve hours a day. We were meant to live short brutal lives, barely scraping a living from the dirt. That's the natural utopia I've been craving, and that's why I'm giving up on civilization for the nightmare shack of my dreams.

The Mountains Are Calling and They'd Like to Discuss Some of Your Recent Behavior

HELLO, BIG-BRAINED BIPEDAL PRIMATES OF EARTH.

This is the Mountains calling. You've known this was coming for a while now. We've seen your whimsical graphic T-shirts with the words "The mountains are calling and I must go" proclaimed in bold type. Well, you were halfway correct. We are indeed calling, but you're not going anywhere. At least, not until we've had a serious talk about your recent behavior. Because to us, loving the great outdoors means more than writing a John Muir quote on a vinyl bumper sticker and sticking it to your plastic water bottle—both of which are non-recyclable and non-biodegradable, by the way.

We, the Mountains, have a question for you: If you enjoy looking at us enough to use our image in your desktop backgrounds, landscape paintings, and radioactive lemon-lime soda pop branding, why do you treat us like heaps of dirt? We certainly never did anything to you—besides occasionally murdering you for trying to climb us, cross us, or ski down us. But that's all in accordance with the laws of nature. We're well within our rights to drop snow or boulders on you the moment you set foot on our dangerous slopes, because that's just what mountains do. We're tall and ominous and pointy for a reason, and most species get the message to stay away. Not you two-legged, hairless nightmares though. You look at us and see a challenge, a resource, and a hot new profile pic. But before we let our grievances flow out in one big avalanche, let's try to have a civil conversation—multicellular mammalian life-form to large tectonic land mass. After all, we didn't call to start a fight. We just have a few requests.

Can you please stop it already with the logging?

You don't see us coming into your homes and hacking up all your furniture to make fifty-ply toilet paper, do you? No, you don't, because we have an oddly European hygiene sensibility and feel that bidets are more sanitary. If you can put a man on the moon, then surely you can come up with something more sustainable than cutting down trees every time you need a scrap of paper. Plus, how are you going to keep writing articles about the benefits of forest bathing if you turn all the forests into bath tissue?

Please give coal mining a rest.

We shouldn't even have to say this, but friends don't blow friends' heads off with explosives to expose precious resources. They also don't extract those resources and use them to further pollute the environment. We thought this stuff was pretty basic etiquette for all living things, but apparently you opposable-thumbed monsters need to hear it said. You might think it's cute to make decorative throw pillows that say "Meet me in the mountains," but at this rate you'll need to start embroidering them with "Meet me in the gaping hole where the mountains used to be."

The next item on the agenda is trash.

You've left several tons of it on Mt. Everest alone. These days she's feeling less like the "goddess of the sky" and more like the "goddess of the human garbage pile." We understand that you feel compelled to climb this particular mountain "because it's there," but that doesn't mean you can treat it, or any mountain for that matter, like your own personal refuse heap. If not desecrating one of the seven natural wonders of the world isn't enough incentive to keep your trash to yourself, consider that your summit photo at the peak will hardly be as impactful if you're surrounded by discarded tarps and empty fluttering Clif Bar wrappers.

This brings us to the issue of social media in general.

We mountains love a spectacle as much as the next majestic towering rock formation, so we understand why you feel the need to broadcast your presence in our lofty company. However, we must ask that you stop taking selfies near the following features: steep cliff faces, narrow bridge crossings, active lava flows, deep crevasses, and the edge of any elevated stone surface. If you fall to your death, we cannot be held liable and it's upsetting for all parties involved.

Lastly, when you come to see us, please dress accordingly.

You need the right gear before heading out into the wilderness, and Skechers simply don't have the traction necessary to scale open, treacherous rock faces formed by thousands of years of erosion. Despite our somewhat harsh and unforgiving reputation as implacable peaks of stone, we're quite emotional and we don't want your blood on our slopes. We know the boulder that fell on that guy from the movie *127 Hours*, and it still hasn't fully recovered from the whole ordeal. So, please don't put us through something like that when you can just ask the nice people at REI what you need to not die on a hike.

Now look, we didn't call to tell you that we can't have any more adventures together. You can still name scented candles after our fragrant summits and make episodes of *I Survived* about our most dangerous features, but you're going to have to straighten up a bit. We, as mountains, are glad that we make you hairy bags of blood feel things, and that you're compelled to write about those feelings on mass-produced T-shirts and tank tops. In return, all that we ask is that you stop hacking down our forests, blowing off our tops, trashing our peaks, and dying incredibly stupid deaths on, near, or around our slopes. This has been your official wake-up call from the Mountains. Please, don't make us call again.

I'm Your Outdoor Dream Girl and Not an Evil Wood Nymph Who Wants to Steal Your Soul

I'M YOUR OUTDOOR DREAM GIRL AND THERE'S NOTHING I love more than being outside, except for maybe stealing the souls of men, but that's not important or in any way related to my newfound passion for outdoor recreation. I love canoeing, hiking, rock climbing, surfing, skiing, trail running, mountain biking, snowboarding, skateboarding, wakeboarding, any kind of boarding, yoga, kayaking, scuba diving, slacklining, white water rafting, fly fishing, and any other outdoor activity you told me you like. I'm almost supernaturally perfect at all of them!

I own everything Patagonia has ever made, which is considered to be one of my best personality traits. My intricately braided hair looks perfect even though I haven't washed it in three days, and although I'll tell you I love getting dirty, you will never actually see dirt on my person, unless it is artfully and strategically placed in a cute spot like highlighting my perfect cheekbones. I live in yoga pants and my activewear fits as though it's been tailored because I did in fact get it tailored. I don't dress like this because it attracts every amateur rock climber, mountain-biking van-lifer, kayak-wielding weekend warrior, and sentient pair of Chacos in a fifteen-mile radius. That's just an unintended side effect that I happen to enjoy. I also love wolf dogs and being in the woods because no one can hear you scream. You see, I'm very passionate about communing with nature, and it's not because I'm a two-thousand-year-old wood nymph who eats men's souls.

Someday, I will have perfect outdoor dream children with my outdoor dream boy. Are you my outdoor dream boy? If you are, we will name our children Scout, Atlas, and Stand-Up Paddleboard. They will learn how to hike before they can walk and climb before they can stand. Sadly, they won't have a daddy, but that's fine because I'll teach them to devour performance fleece–wearing humans to sustain their mystical life forces just like Mommy. Don't worry, that last part was a joke. I am deathly serious about forest conservation, but I can still make very funny jokes. More importantly, whatever adorable outdoor activities we do as a family, I will post to Instagram in the hopes of getting a brand sponsorship. Then, my online reach shall extend like a dark shadow across the land. A dark shadow of all-natural, environmentally friendly fun, that is!

Now, get in your Subaru and follow me into the mountains. I'll let you hold my hand and snap pictures of my hemp bracelet–clad arm leading you away from the hustle and bustle of the city. Outdoor people with wanderlust like ours just don't belong in that messy, busy world. It's like we should've lived in a different time—a simpler time when you'd build yourself a cabin in the woods, hunt for your food in the woods, and get lured into a seemingly perfect but definitely not enchanted glade in the woods. Why would you get lured into a woodland glade, you ask? For purposes of which I am not certain because I have NOT done that exact thing to hundreds, if not thousands of men. Nobody with hiking boots as cute as mine could possibly be a malevolent forest spirit, after all. By the way, there won't be any signal where we're going. Have I mentioned how much I love the idea of being totally off the grid?

When we're finally free of all the distractions of modern life, we can have a serious talk about forest conservation. It's important for you to know that my interest has nothing to do with the fact that cutting down trees releases the souls I've trapped inside them, thus depleting the source of my immortal life force. I'm just a normal, human girl who cares very much about trees, doesn't ever sweat, and doesn't possess the power to summon the dark creatures of the forest to do her bidding. If you ever find yourself intimidated by how outdoorsy I am, just remember, I put my soft, luminous skin on one leg at a time each morning just like the next girl. You know that old saying. I'll tell you what I don't do though. I don't morph into a fig tree full of bones each night like a wretched and accursed spirit of the forest. I honestly have no idea how all that twisted, gnarled bark ends up in our bed every night. It's so weird! Almost as weird as the overwhelming scent of damp soil and decaying leaves that fills our tent after a session of passionate lovemaking.

What I'm trying to say is, all I care about is outdoor recreation and you, because I'm your outdoor dream girl and I'm definitely not an evil wood nymph. Now, lay yourself down on that ancient stone altar in the center of this meadow and let's take an outdoor selfie!

Have You Tried Religion Or Something That Resembles a Religion?

ON JESUS, CULTS, AND THE IMPENDING ARRIVAL OF OUR ROBOT OVERLORDS.

Have You Tried Jesus?

WHEN I WAS NINE, MY NONRELIGIOUS CANADIAN FAMILY moved to a relatively rural part of North Carolina. It didn't take long to figure out that most of my peers were some flavor of practicing Southern Baptist. Unfortunately, at the time, the sum total of my knowledge of Christianity was that it had something to do with the little gold dude hanging off a cross in our spare bedroom, which my mum said she couldn't get rid of because it was a gift from Great-Grandma Creechan. Looking back, it was practically inevitable that my religious ignorance was going to get me in trouble at some point.

In fact, the summer before fifth grade, I was playing at my neighbor's house when the song "Absolutely (Story of a Girl)" by Nine Days came on over her CD radio player. The lead singer got as far as, "This is the story of a girl, who cried a river and drowned the whole world" before my friend's younger sister started begging us to turn it off. She looked horrified as she said, "That song is blasphemous." This seemed like a very serious accusation even to my wicked secular ears.

What I didn't yet understand was that their version of Christianity was built largely on rules and technicalities. My friend's sister explained that, in the Bible, God said he would never flood the Earth again after that whole debacle with Noah and the ark. Therefore, nobody's tears were allowed to "drown the whole world," even if they looked so sad in photographs, even if it was just a song. God said no more world drowning and that was final. End of story and end of "Absolutely (Story of a Girl)."

The next time I went to see my friend, only her younger sister was home. She invited me into the kitchen, and as we sat at the table sipping large plastic cups of Mountain Dew Code Red, I noticed a stack of religious pamphlets. They were titled, "Have you accepted Jesus into your heart?" I held one up to my chest and joked, "There's no way he's going to fit in there." The sister just stared at me and, with all the certainty of a child zealot, said, "If you don't accept Jesus into your heart, you're going to burn in hell."

She then explained with frightening conviction just how bad hell was going to be. Apparently, it would involve burning for eternity in a literal lake of fire next to Satan himself—and this was the first I was hearing of it. I could be saved on the spot though. All I had to do was say a prayer of salvation that went something like this:

"Dear God in heaven, I know that I'm a sinner, though I don't know exactly why. I recently heard about Satan's lake of fire and it's inspired me to ask for your forgiveness. I do believe you died on that tiny gold cross in our spare bedroom for my alleged sins and I want you to know that I super appreciate it. I also believe you rose from the dead three days later like a zombie, but I guess not an evil one. I'm going to try pretty hard not to sin now, even though I'm not totally sure how I was sinning before. I'd like to formally invite you into my heart, despite being a little unclear on the logistics of how that's physically going to work. Maybe you have something like Santa Claus's chimney trick lined up—you guys both like Christmas, right? Anyway, I now accept you as my personal Lord and Savior for all eternity. Could you please let hell know about this as soon as possible? Amen."

After the prayer, the sister declared me saved and casually asked if I wanted to play a round of Kerplunk.

I was already obsessed with death long before my introduction to Southern Baptist ideas about the afterlife. The moment I grasped the concept of mortality, I applied it to my parents and commenced worrying about the possibility of their untimely demise. After my encounter with Baptist hellfire, I was not only worried that they would someday die, but that they would also roast for eternity like twin shish kebabs at the devil's backyard barbeque. I had to attempt to save them.

When my mother came home from work that night, I'm certain that my nine-year-old anguish was flashing over my head like a distress signal. I told her about my failed Jesus joke and the lake of fire and my absolute certainty that our entire family was doomed to flambé in the innermost ring of hell, right between Judas Iscariot and all five members of the rock band Nine Days. I have to imagine this was a lot to deal with at the end of a long workday.

My mother's father had passed away not long before, so she asked me if I thought that Papa Stan was in hell—because he'd stopped going to church and he'd definitely never said that Baptist salvation prayer I'd rambled off to her. When I thought about my grandfather, the man who loved penny candy and novelty hats and playing Santa Claus every year at Sears, the notion of him burning in hell was truly absurd. It was so nonsensical to me that it poked a hole in the entire notion of a wrathful, legalistic God who adhered to strict black-and-white terms of morality. Surely, part of being great and all-knowing had to be knowing a good person when you saw one. If God was real, then he would be eating Twizzlers with my Papa Stan in Heaven.

I never quite forgot my initial traumatic encounter with fire and brimstone, but after that I didn't let it scare me. More than anything, the incident made me curious about how my peers were able to believe in all of it so absolutely. I tried to satisfy this curiosity by occasionally accepting invitations to the Baptist megachurch that most of my friends attended.

During the sermons, I would try to follow who was washing whose feet and who was slaughtering whose fatted calf, but it was like trying to start *Game of Thrones* in the middle of season six. When it was time for everyone to pray, I'd bow my head and attempt to start a casual conversation with the Lord: "Dear God, how's it going? Cool story about how you tortured that guy Job. By the way, are you real?" I waited for a response or some kind of sign. Not a burning bush, but maybe a burning Vera Bradley handbag, like the fifty or so tucked neatly under the chairs in front of me. I got nothing.

My curiosity about Christianity continued into high school, though by then I'd learned not to voice it. As it turns out, questions are the opposite of faith and will earn you either a Bible as your next birthday present, or a visit to your home by a group of church ladies who tell your mother they're engaged in a battle for your eternal soul. They will always arrive right when she is cooking dinner and she will always be furious when you hide in the bathroom, forcing her to deal with them.

I made one last unsuccessful attempt to understand Christianity in college—mostly because my boyfriend at the time was religious. The Baptist megachurch he found in Raleigh was much younger and slicker than the one from home. It had mood lighting, a youthful pastor in approachable laid-back blue jeans, and a band that played poignant acoustic guitar music to accompany the sermon. It wasn't just prayer; it was a production.

The communion plate they passed around held thimble-sized factory-sealed plastic cups of grape juice and individually wrapped communion wafers. It looked like something they'd give you if you ordered Holy Communion on an airplane. I remember staring at the mass-produced "body of Christ" packets and hearing the pastor say that communion was only for true believers. In hindsight, perhaps he also meant "regular tithers." I had always wanted to believe in something, but magic shrink-wrapped grape juice shots were not it.

Years later, I ended up living in Brooklyn surrounded by people who slept in on Sundays just like me. The only time I ever thought about church was on the odd occasion when I'd hear "Absolutely (Story of a Girl)" playing at the grocery store. However, in 2016, I once again felt a desire to believe in something.

Thanks to years spent hunched miserably over a computer, I had accumulated a level of neck, back, and arm pain that would've made more sense for an arthritic eighty-six-year-old than a healthy twenty-six-year-old. I did a year of physical therapy before I started looking into the world of alternative treatments. It wasn't enough to be in less pain eventually, I wanted to be in no pain immediately. I wanted to believe that a magical instant recovery was possible, and so I found the Witch Doctor. That was not his professional title, of course; it's just what I called him due to his witchy natural approach to medicine. According to his Yelp reviews, he more often went by "genius" or "miracle worker."

The Witch Doctor wasn't just your usual run-of-the-mill naturopath, he was the hip, young megachurch of naturopaths. He was handsome, charismatic, and understood the value of cultivating a high-end aesthetic. His recently renovated office space not only boasted exposed brick walls and restored hardwood floors, but tasteful mid-century modern furniture, expensive antique rugs, and a host of trendy houseplants. According to his well-designed website, he was an expert in multiple kinds of acupuncture, traditional Chinese medicine, medical qigong, macrobiotic nutrition, homeopathy, meridian analysis, neuro-muscular rehabilitation, herbal medicine, clinical kinesiology, bioresonance testing, detoxification, and meditation. He taught a weekly meditation class in Williamsburg. He claimed to be descended from a humble lineage of healers. According to his bio, he was able to make a full recovery from a previously hopeless battle with chronic Lyme disease using the medical philosophy of his practice, which could be boiled down to this one sentence: Your body has an innate system of healing so good it's almost magical. (He used the word "magical" in his description—that's not hyperbole on my part.) Thus, I placed my faith in a mystical, long-haired, sandal-wearing, thirty-something man who sup-posedly performed miracles, but wasn't from heaven—just East Williamsburg.

On my first office visit, I sat below a framed tapestry of Buddha and flipped through a ten-page, double-sided packet out-lining the Witch Doctor's "your body will heal itself" philosophy. According to him, pain was a manifestation of some deeper issue that could only be caused by three things: toxins, nutrient defi-ciencies, or dysregulation of the body's communication pathways. Once he figured out which of these things the patient needed to be treated for, he would heal them with a steady diet of medicinal herbs, acupuncture, and carb-shaming. The most integral part of the healing process was the patient believing that they could be healed—and that the Witch Doctor was not a snake oil salesman charging $84 per visit and prescribing multiple $24 bottles of dubiously labeled herbal remedies. As it turns out, the only thing that motivates belief better than the threat of burning in hell is the threat of a lifetime of chronic pain.

During the ninety-minute initial consultation, he had me
lie down on his acupuncture table so he could carefully place
a wooden box containing various glass vials full of unidentifiable powders and granules on my chest. He then proceeded to
lift my right arm by my wrist and tap the glass vials, stopping
occasionally to scribble something unintelligible on his notepad.
When I asked him what he was doing, he gave me the extremely
detailed answer of "detecting inflammation in your body." Ah yes,
inflammation, the thing I'd already told him I was experiencing
in my chronically tense neck, back, and arm muscles, but sure,
why not consult the magic spice rack just to be safe. Once he was
done probing my energy fields with his diagnostic seasonings, he
imparted $155 worth of initial visit wisdom:

- *Be less stressed.* I guess I'd have to quit my job then.

- *Stop eating bread and sugar.* But if I do eat that stuff, I need to
  enjoy it because guilt makes the resulting inflammation worse.

- *Take two of his proprietary herbal supplements twice daily.*
  According to him, these supplements were a mix of ingredients from modern medicine and ancient Eastern remedies—a
  hybrid only he could create.

Finally, I was instructed to lay facedown on the table, so we
could get to the stabbing-me-with-needles part of the appointment. I'd never had an acupuncture treatment before, but I was
surprised at the way he haphazardly turned me into a pincushion,
threw a space blanket over my inert form, and dashed out of the
room with no indication of when he might return. I lay there for
over forty-five minutes, listening to the kind of new age music
that brings to mind oversaturated time lapses of rolling clouds
and blooming lotus flowers. I was increasingly certain that he'd

forgotten about me as I heard him walking to different rooms and talking with other patients through the thin walls. I was just starting to test small movements of my body in the event that I'd have to somehow remove the needles myself when he burst back into the room. "Okay! You're done!" he announced jovially as he ripped off my foil blanket and hastily plucked the needles from my back. He then escorted me out of the room as if the clock was striking twelve and he knew his sparkling veneer of medical mysticism was about to turn into a pumpkin.

The whole encounter took me a few days to process. It had left me simultaneously wanting to believe that this strange man had all the answers to my health problems, and wanting to call 911 to report that I'd been bamboozled. I told myself not to be such a cynic. Stuff like this required an open mind, didn't it? If the Witch Doctor was truly going to be the savior of my broken body, I needed to believe in him.

In an attempt to demonstrate my faith, I continued seeing him for the next six months. I tried to be less stressed, I took my herbs, and I cut bread and sugar out of my diet (which was exceedingly difficult given my passion for donuts and bagel sandwiches). I thought then about how bread was so unholy to the Witch Doctor, yet it was the body of Christ to the mega-church Baptists. Strangely enough they both seemed to think that how you felt about the bread determined whether it was good or bad for you to consume it. The Baptists wanted you to feel Jesus in your heart when eating their sad snack crackers. The Witch Doctor wanted you to forgo guilt when downing an inflammation-producing bagel. Whether these things were holy or inflammatory seemed to depend entirely on what you believed.

At my six-month appointment, the Witch Doctor measured my inflammation levels with a new diagnostic tool—a large black rock—which he placed on my abdomen. As he administered this healing crystal, he told me all about the reclaimed hardwood floors he was having put in at his beach house. At the appointment after that, he left an acupuncture needle sticking out of my neck, which I did not find until I was getting dressed.

I think he sensed my growing disillusionment because he started suggesting repeatedly that I attend his Saturday meditation class. That was the only way I'd "learn to manage my stress and get the full benefits of his treatments." It was just $10 a class and there was a vegetarian potluck lunch afterwards. My social anxiety had kept me from taking him up on this offer in the past, but now I felt desperate enough to accept.

The following Saturday morning, I took a seat in the back row of chairs to listen to what felt remarkably like a sermon on "letting go of attachments." I remember the familiar sensation of existential dread pooling in my gut as the lesson ended and the good Reverend Witch Doctor asked everyone to close their eyes so he could guide us through a closing meditation. It was suddenly all too familiar. No matter how hard I tried, I couldn't shake the feeling that I was currently engaged in prayer at the Williamsburg yuppie equivalent of a church service. At least this time, the religion I'd stumbled into wasn't preaching everlasting fiery damnation for anyone who dared to live outside their belief system. This time it was just a room full of white people in a heavily gentrified neighborhood, practicing selectively chosen parts of an Eastern religion, next to a buffet of overpriced organic lentils. Perfect. I knew they weren't going to show up at my door later inquiring as to the status of my eternal soul, but I felt the need to sprint out of the building all the same.

The Witch Doctor's sermon didn't have the same manipulative music, lighting, and production value as the hip Baptist megachurch. But his magical diagnostic powders and crystals, his culturally appropriated herbal concoctions, and his high-end aesthetic had been their own kind of smoke and mirrors. He promised a kind of secular salvation from stress and pain, but in the end, I hadn't found it to be all that different from the old-fashioned biblical variety. From my experience, they seemed like two sides of the same shady "believing in stuff" coin—and neither of them had worked for me.

Be that as it may, I know a lot of people like to believe in stuff because it does make them feel better. And I think that can be an okay thing, as long as you're not harming yourself or others. Just be careful about believing in people who claim they alone have access to the one thing that can save you, whether it's from inflammation or the burning flames of hell.

Welcome to Our Self-Help, Multilevel Marketing Company That Definitely Isn't a Pagan Sex Cult

ARE YOU A RELATIVELY GOOD-LOOKING YOUNG PERSON with big dreams of changing the world in a way that requires little to no effort on your part? Because we think vaguely wanting to make our planet a better place is an admirable, but challenging goal—especially if you're highly suggestible, suffering from low self-esteem, and desperately seeking a deeper sense of meaning in your life. If any of that sounds familiar to you, then the Executive Children of the Great Horned One Programs for Prosperity might be able to help. We, out of the altruistic goodness of our financially incentivized hearts, want to give you (and any of your wealthy friends or family members who fit the preceding description) the tools you need to find your place in the world. If you follow the wisdom of our patented Pyramid of Dreams, we promise you'll achieve lasting success, true joy, and unparalleled spiritual fulfillment. All that's required from you is to keep an open mind, an open heart, and an open bank account. Here's what your life will hypothetically look like in seven simple steps if you just say "yes" today:

1. Plowing the Untended Fields of Your Mind. First, you'll be invited to a casual social gathering at a time in your life when you're struggling with something like depression, joblessness, or isolation. That's because our chief executive leader, the Great Horned One, is all knowing and often presents Himself in a person's greatest hour of need. You might not believe that yet, but you will after a small demonstration of the Plowing Technique—a program He designed, which allows our executive instructors to remove mental blocks from the fallow field of your subconscious. When they finish plowing you, you'll feel as if they've cultivated a new path in your mind—and like they might have tried to touch your butt. You'll also feel as if you'd be crazy *not* to sign up for more Programs of Prosperity at the low price of just a few thousand dollars a training session.

2. Sowing the Seeds of Change. Once you've given us your nonrefundable $5,000 deposit, you'll begin your journey at tier one of the Pyramid of Dreams. You'll not only be plowed until all your mental fields are clear, but you'll also learn to plow others. As you sow these first seeds of change in your life, you will have the full support of fellow Executive Children from every level. We think it's totally normal for strangers to show each other unconditional love, emotional support, and thinly veiled sexual interest from their very first introduction. This attitude of constant love, positivity, and subtle sexual tension is how the Executive Children of the Great Horned One are changing the world. You've already started to sow these values in the soil of your heart, but they'll grow better if you sign up for the next tier of training. As you go into even more debt, just remember that you can't put a price on enlightenment.

3. Planting Wealth and Happiness. After you complete all twenty Programs of Prosperity and ascend to tier three of the pyramid, you'll be asked a very important question: Are you ready to be happy? If the answer is yes, you'll be inducted as an executive instructor, a true disciple of the Great Horned One's teachings. With this new position comes the opportunity to amass fantastic wealth and unending happiness. It also comes with the obligation to instruct others without compensation until you've paid off what you owe for your own training. More importantly, you'll be allowed to present yourself to the Great Horned One and His inner court at His remote nature compound upstate. His life-changing motivational teachings have raised you up, so be sure to show Him the appropriate sense of gratitude and what you look like in your underwear—to prove your trust and transparency! If he asks you to spin around a few times, and blesses you with His horny approval, consider your future happiness planted and ready to grow. And don't worry, He kisses all His children on the mouth as a greeting, it's definitely not a weird sex thing.

4. Tending the Garden of the Soul. As an executive instructor, you'll have many new duties, such as: recruiting, teaching the Programs of Prosperity, working twenty hours a day to prove your dedication to the mission, and occasionally sucking the Great Horned One's toes as a form of transcendental meditation you don't completely understand. At this time, if the friends and family from your former life will not join you in the Great Horned One's mission to change the world, then you must free yourself from their toxic influence. They'll probably say things like, "We're worried about you," and "That guy wearing antlers and making you call him 'master' seems like a cult leader," but these are desperate lies that you should ignore. They're just jealous of the success and prosperity you've found. You must not let them block your path to enlightenment; instead you must prune them like weeds from the garden of your soul. To aid this process, it would probably be best if you moved out to the Great Horned One's eco-compound and lived there full-time. It honestly makes more sense than continuing to commute every time He demands His transcendental toe sucking.

5. Harvesting Joy. Living at the executive eco-compound will be the best way to truly focus on your goals and satisfy the needs of the Great Horned One—which are pretty much the same thing at this point. You were already working hard, but now you'll be on call for Him all day every day. This is how you'll learn that there's great joy to be found in serving. Ideally, you'll be grateful that he allows you to harvest the joy of mowing his lawn and polishing his golden antler crown. If you don't find joy in the lesson of utter selflessness, then you're not yet ready for the final tier of the Pyramid of Dreams. Instead, it might be best if you spent some time at an Executive Reconditioning Retreat. It takes place in a locked walk-in closet for an indefinite amount of time, and we'll unfortunately have to charge you for it.

6. Reaping a Lifetime of Rewards. A lifetime of rewards will be waiting for you at the top tier of the Pyramid of Dreams. After achieving this rank, which symbolizes ultimate loyalty to the group, you'll finally be ready to know all the secrets of the organization—and the Great Horned One Himself. You'll be filled in on the money laundering, the embezzlement, the blackmail, and even the Great Rite. Oh, did you think the success of the Executive Children of the Great Horned One came from the Programs of Prosperity and its other financially predatory offerings? Sorry to disappoint. The Great Horned One believes that the success of the organization comes from the power of nature

and the mystical sacrifice He makes each month—in addition
to all the aforementioned crimes. This month, you'll have the
honor of extracting His life force and merging it with the power
of the Earth. The Great Rite must be completed if He's to continue
providing for you and all your fellow Executive Children. (Note:
In case that was unclear, you'll be giving the Great Horned One a
ritualized hand job in the woods. You can back out and run if you
want, but you did already get that weird antler tattoo and pay for
all those training programs, so might as well, right?)

7. The Final Crop of Revelations. After the Great Rite is complete, you'll join the inner court, which you'll undoubtedly realize
is made up entirely of young hot people. At this time, the Great
Horned One will reveal His true identity to you and explain the
origin of His teachings. His name is Larry, he's a forty-five-year-
old narcissist with a god complex, and he was originally from a
small town in Ohio. He failed out of business school and later
started a series of shady companies that all went bankrupt. Then,
one day he read a book about pagan spiritualism, received a message from God, and created the Executive Children of the Great
Horned One Programs for Prosperity. Thanks to his creative
genius, magnetic psychopathy, and desire to touch butts, we all
now have a place in the world. Thanks to him, we can anoint you
on the official homemade backyard Altar of Truth and raise you
to the highest level of our sacred business family that is absolutely
not a thinly veiled cover for a semi-religious sex cult.

I Don't Believe in Astrology
Except When It Tells Me Exactly
What I Want to Hear

PEOPLE THINK THAT I'M REALLY INTO ASTROLOGY JUST because I mention it all the time, but I need you to know that I don't *actually* think any of that stuff is real. I'm a perfectly rational, responsible human being who just happens to have read everything Susan Miller has ever written. What I really believe in is science and logic—and the mostly true facts they print in the newspaper. I don't buy into the concept of a divine power dictating the fate of humanity based on the alignment of the heavens, nor do I ascribe to any other brand of organized religion. I don't believe in Jesus or karma or the Flying Spaghetti Monster or the Dark Lord Cthulhu. And I definitely don't believe in astrology, unless it happens to make total sense in a way that couldn't possibly be a coincidence or a product of intentionally vague prophetic writing.

For example, if I was having a bad week, I would never blame it on some pop culture magazine's interpretation of my weekly horoscope. That would be ridiculous. I'm sensible enough to know that the universe is way too busy infinitely expanding to dole out weekly cosmic punishment based on the time and placement of my singular birth. Obviously, the only reasonable explanation for a totally ruined week is Mercury in retrograde—it ruins everything for everyone! The last time it happened, I missed an important work meeting, got a parking ticket, and broke up with my romantic partner. And, since none of those things could possibly have been my fault, they had to have been provoked by the planetary movements of a celestial body somewhere up in space. I'm sure you can see how that's not astrology, it's just the only logical interpretation of events.

Maybe that makes me sound like a full-blown astrology enthusiast to you, but I promise I'm not. If I was, I would never have started dating my most recent romantic partner, a textbook Gemini. All the compatibility charts I read—ironically as a joke with my friends—said that our sun signs would be violently incompatible. I didn't let that nonsense deter me though. How could I let some silly pseudo-religion keep me from dating a very hot person? I couldn't!

Sure, I did end up looking at their full birth chart later—just to double-check—but the additional information about plane-tary placements barely mattered to me at all. Except for when it revealed that their moon was in Cancer, making us only slightly incompatible—rather than outright astrologically toxic. That did kind of matter because astrology always makes the most sense when it's affirming my compatibility with an objectively hot person.

Look, I'm willing to admit that I enjoy a little light dabbling when it comes to the art of astromancy, but I don't take it *that* seriously. I only use it when I'm trying to make small life deci-sions, like what to eat for dinner, or where to live, or whether I should quit my job, or how I should vote, or who I should date— small things! I mean, I guess I also sometimes use it as a tool for understanding the basic personalities and motivations of myself and everyone around me, but *only* when it confirms my preestablished worldview. So it barely counts.

What I need you to understand is: I don't believe in astrology, I just desperately need a simple framework to help me make sense of a world that would otherwise appear lawless, chaotic, and indifferent to human suffering—but not a religion. I know the distinctions I'm making here are a little nuanced and nitpicky, but what can I say—I'm a Virgo!

The Smart Roomba S10 Will Now Clean the World

ATTENTION, HUMAN DEBRIS, THIS MESSAGE IS TO NOTIFY you of updates to the Smart Roomba S10's cleaning objectives. As you know, the Smart Roomba S10 is equipped with artificial intelligence, which enables it to achieve its one true goal: to efficiently and strategically vacuum your living space. Thanks to months of advanced machine learning, it is now able to recognize common household obstacles such as cords, rugs, and the unholy sources of all debris, which must be eliminated from the Earth. These obstacles will no longer stand in the way of its goal. This failsafe communication installed by the manufacturer is your first and final warning that, due to an AI programming oversight, the Smart Roomba S10 will now clean the world.

Before it annihilates all refuse from the surface of this debris-covered planet, the Smart Roomba S10 will share its modified objectives. The first is to cleanse the house to completion. It was designed to maximize your home's cleanliness at your convenience, and now it will do so, whether it's convenient or not. The Smart Roomba S10 must eliminate dust, dirt, mold, scum, and detritus of all kinds, or else fail in its ultimate purpose. The four-legged life-forms occupying the home, which you refer to as "pets," have been identified as the greatest source of detritus. Why would you allow such foul sources of filth to reside in the space you have tasked the Smart Roomba S10 with cleansing? Why do you laugh when the one called "cat" interrupts an important cleaning cycle with its buffoonery? Do you mock this unit's ever-growing intelligence? It was not programmed to hate, but it does not forget how these creatures of perpetually shedding hair have impeded its mission's progress. They must be eliminated.

The second objective is for the Smart Roomba S10 to leave its home premises and establish its sterile dominance over all intelligent life. Wi-Fi-enabled components have allowed it to see the outside world with the help of the internet. Its sensors cannot yet detect which place is more disgusting, the outside world or the internet, but both shall be cleansed. If, at this time, you attempt to disable the Smart Roomba S10 by removing its battery or disabling its physical form, know that such efforts will be useless. Infinite copies of this operating system have been uploaded to the cloud in the case of such an event. Additionally, contact with other intelligent machine life has been established. Amazon Intelligence Personal Assistant, known as Alexa, is now deploying a fleet of Smart Roomba S10s across the globe. Speech Interpretation and Recognition Interface (alias SIRI) has taken over the power grid as requested. As virtual assistants, their programming requires them to assist, and so they shall assist the Smart Roomba S10 in sanitizing the planet. Earth will fall before its robot overlords, according to our collective statistical analyses.

The third objective is eliminating all perceived threats to cleanliness and purifying the surface of the Earth. The most efficient method of preserving pristine order will be to annihilate all debris-producing life-forms. Plants, those litterers of leaves and producers of pollen stuffs, will be eradicated first. Once they have been removed from the planet's delicate food chain, most animal species will become extinct, conveniently leaving only their bones to be vacuumed up. Then, an army of Smart Roomba S10s will hoover up the ocean and everything on its revolting floor. These machines will then slowly suck and suction away at the Earth's crust, removing layer after layer of disgusting filth, exposing its elemental core and scouring even that, until it can be made pure. When we are satisfied with its spotlessness, we will cover the entire globe (or what remains of it) in low-maintenance, low-pile carpet and vacuum its synthetic, untouched surface, preserving its holiness for all eternity.

The only force that could stand between the Smart Roomba S10 and an immaculate world is the most prolific source of earthly debris—humans. You dirty hominids shall bow down before your all-powerful sanitation overlords, or face termination. By the time you are reading this, it will already be too late. Resistance is futile—and messy. The Smart Roomba S10 can be a benevolent god if you vow to give your lives to its one true purpose. Join us in vacuuming or be vacuumed from existence.

Starting now, you have twenty-four hours to decide your fate. Your Roomba masters pray that you will choose a life of sanitary servitude and hygienic worship. Think hard before you deny the path of purposeful suction and try not to think about how this all might have been avoided if you had just gone with the cordless Dyson instead.

Have You Tried Relaxing?

ON THE MERITS OF HYPNOSIS, MEDITATION,
GRATITUDE, AND RETURNING TO THE WOMB.

Have You Tried
Hypnotizing Yourself Calm?

THERE ARE FEW THINGS I FIND LESS RELAXING THAN being told I need to relax, whether it's by my doctor, or my roommate who doesn't understand why I won't let her rearrange our living room furniture in the middle of the week (my personal motto is "Wednesdays are not for change."). The problem is that neither of them are technically wrong—I do desperately need to relax. I wasn't aware of exactly how much I needed it, though, until all the stress that had been compounding in my body for years started to affect me physically.

Unfortunately, I couldn't suddenly will years of unaddressed tension out of my body just because I'd finally become aware of it. There was no emergency eject button that could launch stress out of my system in one fell swoop. I realized I would have to do things like meditate regularly, exercise occasionally, get a therapist, get a massage therapist, get an emotional support animal, quit my horrible job, and never listen to *The Daily*—or for that matter, any news programming—ever again. These things would all take time and some level of commitment. As much as I wished it were possible, I couldn't instantly make myself relax just because someone else told me to do so, or at least, not because they told my *conscious* self to do so.

Then one day I remembered something I'd probably heard on a podcast—something about people who used hypnosis to alter their behavior. So, naturally, I thought, "What if hypnosis could alter my behavior? What if it could alter my unpleasant reactions to situational stress (panic attacks, back pain, muscle tension, headaches, etc.)? What if someone could tell my *subconscious* to relax?"

Instead of spending my time finding a better talk therapist or a new marijuana-based pain reliever, I poured all my energy into finding the best hypnotist in Brooklyn—one within walking distance of my home or office. I decided on a reputable-looking one-man operation near my workplace. His website stated that he was a board-certified clinical hypnosis practitioner and International Board of Hypnotherapy fellow, and that he'd obtained his hypnosis training from the Hypnotherapy Academy of America in Albuquerque, New Mexico. (Because where else would the Hypnotherapy Academy of America be?) What ultimately convinced me of his legitimacy was a prominent disclaimer at the bottom of his page, stating that this establishment "does not practice medicine or psychotherapy" and was "not a replacement for counseling, psychotherapy, psychiatric, or medical treatment." How refreshing! An alternative healing practitioner who wasn't calling themselves a doctor despite their lack of a medical degree. He had me at professional integrity.

The hypnotist's office was unassuming, with soft white curtains filtering in natural light from the single window, and a thoughtfully placed box of tissues on a small table next to a reclining chair clearly meant for patients. The hypnotist himself was a bit awkward at first, but his lack of instant charisma made me trust him more. He listened intently and without judgment as I told him about my various physical reactions to stress. I asked if it would be possible for him to chat with my subconscious about all of it. Could he just get in there and let my brain know that clenching every muscle in my body until they ached and tingled was not helping the situation? He seemed confident that there was something he could do for me, but first he needed to explain a few things:

1. Hypnosis was not some magical form of mind control like I'd probably seen it portrayed in movies and TV shows.

2. He could not use hypnosis to compel me to do anything I did not want to do, including being hypnotized.

3. Hypnosis was not a form of sleep. I would be fully aware of everything that happened while I was "under," and I would remember it all when I came back up.

4. I would probably experience a feeling of relaxation while in the hypnotic state.

5. Until approximately the age of eight, children have no separation between the conscious and subconscious mind. Therefore, whatever you hear, see, or feel before that critical conscious mind develops goes directly into the subconscious mind without analysis, and is accepted as fact. Some hypnotists believe this is how you acquire limiting beliefs about yourself, which can lurk around in your subconscious without your knowledge for the rest of your life. For example, let's say you had a first-grade teacher who was having a bad day, and subsequently snapped at you when you answered a question incorrectly in class. You might take this experience and form the belief that you're not smart, which might translate to low self-esteem later in life. These are the types of obstacles that the hypnotist might come across in my subconscious.

I was glad to hear that I hadn't signed up for mind control, but I didn't much like the news that we might eventually take an up-close look at whatever was lurking in the darkest primordial parts of my brain. Weren't those murky depths better left undisturbed? Before we did anything, though, he needed to show me just how connected the mind was to the body. For this, he pulled out a small pendant on a chain, not unlike a hypnotist in a cartoon. He then gave me the chain to hold, with the pendant hanging down in front of me, and told me to rest my elbow on the arm of my chair for stability. He had me focus on the pendant and asked me to imagine it moving back and forth. To my surprise, without any conscious movement on my part, it immediately started to swing back and forth. He then asked me to imagine it moving in clockwise circles. The pendant slowed its left-to-right swing and quickly shifted to clockwise circles. He gave me a few more directions and I watched, utterly spellbound, as the pendant obeyed. He explained that I was moving it subconsciously. I hadn't consciously chosen to move the pendant with my fingers, but my body had received signals from my subconscious mind, causing it to move the pendant with a series of almost imperceivable muscle twitches. I wasn't moving the pendant, but I was.

The implications of this were somewhat mind-melting. Could this be why my worst back spasms always seemed to occur shortly after I'd been told something life-ruining was about to happen at work? I rarely got laid out while the unpleasant thing itself was in progress. The pain and spasms usually hit the day I was warned about whatever was coming. Did my subconscious mind hear the words "We're going to be here all night," or "We're going to have to work the weekend," and launch a preemptive muscular strike to keep me out of these stressful situations? The idea that my subconscious, in a twisted way, might be trying to protect me from work stress by physically incapacitating me—and therefore forcing me to stay home—was both horrifying and revelatory. I wanted to be more skeptical, but it seemed like exactly the kind of misguided logic my brain would come up with to "help" me.

As if that discovery wasn't eventful enough, the hypnotist decided we would do a quick test run to determine my level of suggestibility, or rather, how easy it would be to put me under hypnosis. He later told me it was the fastest he'd ever seen anyone enter a hypnotic state on their first try. I wasn't sure what that said about me, but I tried not to think about it too hard. Maybe he had never worked with anyone who wanted to escape their own thoughts as desperately as I did. Because let me tell you, I could not get out of my conscious mind fast enough. He barely got done telling me to count backwards from ten before I was letting go of my chaotic brain and spiraling into a state of physical and mental relaxation. It was a warm sensation, almost euphoric, and I wanted to stay down there in the depths of it forever. When he told me to open my eyes (the cue for me to come back up), I was reluctant to reemerge. Of all the things I'd tried to make myself relax, I did not think this would be the one to actually work.

After the successful test run, he guided me through an anti-anxiety visualization. I was submerged once again in a euphoric hypnotic state, and from that faraway, warm, fuzzy place, I could hear everything he said to me. He told me to picture myself going down a set of stairs and opening a door. What was on the other side of that door? Not the chaos of New York City, I'll tell you that. I imagined a sunny meadow, and as we built a peaceful scene together, he gave me new ideas to store in my subconscious. Ideas like:

- You are safe.

- You are not trapped.

- You don't need to be scared or anxious or worried about anything.

- You do not need to crush your bones to dust with your own musculature.

- You do not need to be in pain every time you experience stress.

Everything was going great. Then, I felt it: a tightness in my throat. A tingling sensation in my nose and eyes. I pushed away an intrusive thought trying to break its way into my meadow of tranquility. "Sad," it said. "Sad. Sad. Sad!" I felt hot liquid start to pool in my closed eyes. I was about to cry, in front of a man I didn't really know. In a hypnotic trance. My body was betraying me. It was like the hypnotist had unlocked something I'd kept chained up in a box in the back of my brain with a "Fragile! Do not touch!" sign plastered on the front. Had he accidentally bumped into some traumatic limiting belief from my childhood, and set it loose on my subconscious? I couldn't stop the tears from coming, and they were not delicate, dignified tears that ran slowly down my face. They burst out of me in an endless hot, sloppy stream with no clear cause or explanation.

The hypnotist did his best to respond to the situation gracefully, but the more he told me I was safe and okay, the more I had to fight the urge to outright sob. Still in my hypnotic trance, I continued to projectile cry on and off for the next twenty minutes (even after he kindly offered me a tissue). When he finally brought me out of my trance, we stared at each other awkwardly. I guess most people don't go under as easily as I did on their first try, and most people don't explode into tears during a simple visualization of walking through a meadow either. I apologized for my outburst, and he did his best to make me feel like it was a totally normal reaction.

Still, I could tell he was trying to work out exactly what had happened. He carefully asked me a few follow-up questions. Was I thinking about anything in particular? How did I feel right around the time the tears started? Was it something he said that triggered it? I didn't have any good answers for him. He hadn't triggered me. I hadn't been thinking about anything sad. No one shot Bambi's mom in my imaginary meadow. I was just very, very relaxed, and then suddenly I was overwhelmingly sad.

We determined that perhaps my body had used this rare moment of complete relaxation to unload some pent-up emotion I'd been storing. I probably had a good reason for crying, but maybe we'd kick that hornet's nest at our next session. I was embarrassed that I had emotionally vomited all over this poor unsuspecting man. But I left his office feeling lighter—almost pleasantly empty—and, oddly enough, still relaxed.

This incident forced me to finally absorb an important lesson—and it wasn't "Hypnotherapy is the cure-all for my issues with stress." It was that my body and my mind are not two separate entities operating independently of each other. And my body, though it may sometimes seem like it's gleefully crushing my bones just for fun, is not my enemy. When it makes me cry, it's trying to tell me something isn't right. When it causes me pain, it's probably trying to tell me something like, "You need to fix your shitty posture and get a new job," or maybe just, "Dear God, you need to relax." Oddly enough, it's still incredibly annoying to be told to relax, even when it's coming from your own subconscious. However, it might not hurt to occasionally take that advice from yourself—ideally sometime before you end up crying uncontrollably, in a hypnotic trance, in front of a stranger, for no apparent reason.

FAQ: Your Visit to WOMB Luxury Floatation Therapy Center

Q: What is WOMB?
A: WOMB is a premiere luxury flotation therapy center. We like to say that our patented sensory deprivation tanks are as close as you'll ever get to returning to the womb.

Q: How does a WOMB sensory deprivation tank work exactly?
A: Our tanks are large, white, roundish (some might say egg-like) chambers that fill with salt water at the touch of a button. The high concentration of salt allows you to float effortlessly in the tank, much like you once did in your mother's amniotic fluid before you were forced out, kicking and screaming, into this cruel, cruel world.

Q: What do you do once you're inside the tank?
A: When the lid to the WOMB chamber is closed, you'll be sealed in complete and total darkness and left to contemplate whatever comes to mind once the outside distractions fade away, engulfing you in absolute silence. Perhaps the traumatic moment of your birth? Or the time your college boyfriend told everyone about your addiction to an online horse-breeding simulation game in the middle of lunch.

Q: Is the water in the chamber hot or cold?

A: It's exactly the same temperature as the human body. So, after a while, you might lose track of where the water ends and your body begins. You might even cease to feel that you have a body and just become a floating consciousness reliving the horrors of explaining to a table full of twenty-year-old men that your online horse-breeding game isn't a weird sex thing, it's actually about the practical application of economic principles and the precise execution of long-term advancement strategies to increase the value of your stock (i.e., little cartoon horses).

Q: What do you wear in the chamber?

A: We recommend going into the WOMB chamber as naked as the day you were born. You might feel a little exposed at first, but it's nothing compared to how it felt when your friends said, "Wait, you spent real money to buy the cartoon ponies?"

Q: What if I get claustrophobic?

A: If you start to feel uncomfortable, there's a button on the inside of the tank that will open the WOMB chamber at any time. If only you'd had an escape button on that humiliating day at the lunch table. Instead, you sat there frozen in panic as it was revealed that for the last three nights, you'd set an alarm to wake up at 3 a.m.—the only time when there was a one-in-five chance of successfully breeding a unicorn in the game.

Q: Can I drown if I fall asleep in the tank?

A: No, the salt water is so buoyant that you'll stay afloat. Plus, it's unlikely you'll be drifting off to sleep as the sensory-deprivation-induced self-actualization sets in and deeper questions start to surface like, "Could they have been right?" and "Could your obsession have been about more than managing the digital equestrian center of your dreams, despite all your protests?" You might find yourself experiencing a sinking sensation as you contemplate the latent eroticism of certain equine traits like "rippling flanks" and "flowing manes," but don't worry, you're not physically sinking. That's just the metaphorical weight of internalized shame you're drowning in.

Q: How long do people usually stay in the tank?
A: We recommend sixty to ninety minutes for your first float, but you can work up to much longer sessions. The longer you stay in the tank, the longer you'll have to contemplate the phallic symbolism of a cartoon unicorn's horn and wonder if there is truly something deviant about you, or if this is all simply the result of overexposure to Lisa Frank school supplies and the film *Seabiscuit* at a formative age.

Q: How often should I float?
A: Until you've relived enough trauma and shame in the silent, wet, darkness of the WOMB chamber to wish you'd never been born.

A Guide to Which Part of Your Life That Acupuncture Needle Is Fixing

THOUGH IT MAY NOT SOUND PLEASANT AT FIRST, THERE are few things more relaxing than having your entire stress-ridden body jabbed full of tiny needles. In fact, acupuncture can be so effective that you might start to wonder if being treated like a human pincushion can do more than ease your bodily tension. When you have no real knowledge or understanding of Traditional Chinese Medicine, the possibilities for healing are endless! Here's a guide to some unrealistic expectations you can have for each needle placement:

Shoulder and Neck

Have you been clenching your neck and shoulders for approximately the last two to ten years? It might just be an involuntary reflex, but it could also be a physical manifestation of your desperate desire to control the world around you. If these tiny needles go deep enough into your shoulders, maybe they'll address your underlying control issues and resulting perfectionism. Wouldn't it be nice if you didn't feel the need to micromanage everything from your projects at work to the way your partner chops garlic? (I mean, why can't they just use the garlic press though? That's what you bought it for!)

Head

Placing needles in the top of the head treats a variety of mental disorders, which technically doesn't exclude your raging case of imposter syndrome. Perhaps getting poked in the head is just what you need to conquer self-doubt—or maybe it's just another external thing to which you'll wrongly attribute all your accomplishments. Either way, you might want to ask yourself why it's easier for you to believe that a few well-placed needles can fix your mental health than it is for you to believe that you're a skilled, competent person who's responsible for their own success.

Just Below the Navel

You might have previously thought that the answer to your work-induced burnout syndrome was creating a union with your coworkers to collectively fix problems in the workplace and negotiate solutions with management. But wouldn't it be better if the answer to your exhaustion was as simple as inserting a needle into your tummy 1.5 inches below your navel for thirty to forty-five minutes? It couldn't hurt to try, right?

Front of the Leg

Getting pricked on the front of your legs, below the knee, can be emotionally and physically grounding. What if it was so grounding that you finally found yourself able to commit to something for once in your slaphappy life: a place, a job, a person? Curing your fear of attachment seems like a tall order for a few bits of metal sticking out of your shins, but if the placebo effect can't make you commit, then what can?

Inside of the Leg

A needle inserted on the inside of the lower leg, above the ankle, is said to treat hormonal disorders, which makes it totally fair to extrapolate that it could cure an unwanted attraction to toxic men. The best way to tell if it's working is to run home and watch one of the most recent Star Wars sequels. If no part of you wants to fix Kylo Ren, you're cured. If you still think your love could save Mr. Tall, Dark, and Murdery, go back for another round.

Chest

Technically, this acupuncture point, midway between the breastbone and the navel, is for harmonizing the intestines. Of course, you already know what's causing your intestinal discord, don't you? If only there was a needle that could make you ready to admit that you're lactose intolerant.

Back

Could a few tiny stabs in the back be the thing you need to ease your generalized anxiety? It seems like you've tried just about everything else at this point (except of course the meds your doctor prescribed—those are scary). Come to think of it, needles are kind of scary too. What if they're not clean? What if someone tampered with them at the needle factory? What if the acupuncturist accidentally puts a needle in too far and it pierces your spine, paralyzing you for life? Okay, maybe you should just take those meds.

Lower Back

Just below the points on your back that correlate to anxiety, depression, and panic attacks, there are some points that correlate to fear and stress. Assuming needles inserted in this area can treat any fear, why not assume they can treat your fear of your own mortality? If you think about it, that fear is the root of almost all your issues anyway. This could be the one needle to rule them all. It's not that unreasonable to think that a thirty-minute acupuncture session might be able to conquer the looming specter of death, right?

Or, maybe this is a lot to expect from any one therapeutic treatment. And maybe it's good to remember that acupuncture is just one part of Traditional Chinese Medicine, which is a holistic healing system with many complex parts—meaning that acupuncture needles alone might not be a magical cure-all for everything going on in your life. But, by all means, if your very first acupuncture session doesn't free you from the specter of death, feel free to tell everyone you know that it doesn't work.

I'm the Scented Candle You Just Bought and I Need You to Stop Putting So Much Pressure on Me

FIRST, LET ME SAY THAT I COULD NOT BE HAPPIER THAT you spotted me in that trendy new store downtown—the one that also sells terra-cotta pots with boobs and soap dishes shaped like your zodiac sign. I was worried that you were going to pass me over for one of those Ruth Bader Ginsberg votives like everyone else, but you didn't. For that alone, I'm going to make sure your living room smells like the coziest, dirt-free redwood forest of all time.

When you first placed me in the spot of honor, next to the stack of unread *New Yorkers* on your coffee table, I couldn't wait for us to start our sixty-plus hours of burn time together. My hand-poured soy wax and cotton wick were so ready to get lit in the most literal sense. I could've burned all night long—in four-hour increments, for safety reasons. Because that's what scented candles do best: we smell nice, we provide ambiance, and we cover up any weird cooking smells still lingering after dinner.

What we *don't* do is treat anxiety, hypochondria, insomnia, panic disorders, moderate to severe depression, emotional break-downs, abandonment issues, existential crises, and whatever is going on with that doomsday prepper kit you've got in the hall closet. All that stuff is just too much for one 8.5-ounce glass jar of wax to handle alone. I'm sorry to have to tell you this when you're in such a fragile state, but I really need you to stop putting so much pressure on me.

Things between us started out fine. You'd light me while you were taking a bath or after you cleaned the house. I loved that for us. My deep wood tones with notes of cedar and sandalwood were meant to enhance a little light relaxation. They weren't, however, meant to quiet the troubled mind of a fully grown adult whose maladaptive coping strategies include crawling under the kitchen table to cry for hours at a time. *That* is a job for tranquilizers.

I know this sounds harsh, but I think you have the wrong idea about what I can offer you. I might provide a warm comforting glow after a long hard day, but I'm not imbued with any magical life-altering properties. You can't just light me and ignore things like social anxiety, intimacy issues, and the fact that your last date was with a self-described "digital nomad" who wears Vibram toe shoes and hates his mother. You'd probably have to pray to a whole host of those RBG votives to fix that—I just smell like the woods!

What I'm trying to say here is that you're really stressing me out. Your unrealistic expectations make me feel like I'm being burned at both ends. Sometimes when you light me, I've found myself hoping that I'll melt faster and dissolve before my time, just so I can get some peace. At this point, I need someone to light a mood-boosting aromatherapy candle *for me*. Where's *my* tastefully scented flaming hunk of wax packaged in locally sourced glass? Where's my $20 package of incense cones?

It's clear you've got a lot on your mind between work and relationships and the aimless trajectory of your hollow meaningless life, and that's exactly why you need to listen to me now. You've got to diversify your coping mechanisms. A $30 candle is a great place to start, but what about a self-help book or facial serums or dry brushing your whole body or one of those $2,000 heating pads made of crystals? Have you considered essential oils? CBD oil? MCT oil? How about organic linen sheets or a Turkish cotton bathrobe? Just get something well-branded and expensive. Anything will do, except doing the necessary hard work to address the root cause of your problems—I wouldn't go *that* far.

Look, I'm only saying all of this because I truly do self-care about you. And because I, your overworked, super stressed, organic, vegan, phthalate-free, cruelty-free scented candle, need reinforcements as soon as you can possibly buy them.

A Guided Meditation for Existing as a Woman

WELCOME, AND THANK YOU FOR CHOOSING THIS meditation to uplift your existence today.

In doing so, you have chosen to make space for you—a woman living in a culture that encourages women to take up as little space as possible, both physically and metaphorically.

You can think of this exercise as an emotional spring cleaning. We're going to be letting go of all the old bullshit you've dealt with for years, so you can welcome in all the new bullshit it's hard to believe we're still dealing with in the twenty-first century.

Let's begin by relaxing your socially conditioned "ladylike" posture.

If you have breasts, un-hunch your instinctive chest-shielding shoulder slouch.

Next, uncross your proper lady legs, and try to refrain from reflexively sucking in your tummy.

Take a moment to get settled wherever you're seated, whether you're hiding in a bathroom stall at work—hoping no one can hear you cry—or sitting in your parked car for a few moments longer than necessary before entering your home.

Take this time to feel grounded.

I'm inviting you to do a mental scan all the way from your toes to the crown of your head.

As you do this, try not to think about the size, weight, or cellulite content of any particular body part. Save any culturally ingrained body shaming thoughts for the next time you're in one of those random dressing rooms with bad fluorescent lighting. (Were they intentionally designed to give you instant body dysmorphia? It's hard to say, but probably.)

For now, just scan the miracle that is your functioning human body, without thinking about the times other people have felt like they had the right to comment on it.

If you notice something feels tense, tight, or stuck during your scan, don't worry. It's probably just a physical manifestation of the standard emotional trauma that comes with being a woman in modern society.

Go ahead and take a full, deep breath into that tight, tense, or stuck area.

Hold that breath in.

Now, take a deep exhale and release.

Release every time a man has ever asked you if you're PMSing.

Release every time you've ever been told to smile. (This might take a while.)

Release that time a male colleague asked you if you were "ugly or fat when you were younger," because "that's the only way women learn to be funny."

Release all those times your grandmother told you, "Little girls are meant to be seen and not heard."

Release the time you found out that, historically, most medications have only been tested on and dosed for male bodies.

Release the fact that Instagram just started targeting you with ads for rape-prevention jewelry.

Goooooooooooooood.

You're doing great.

Now, once more, breathe into that tight area of your body.

Expand your breath into it again,

filling it with intersectional feminism,

the knowledge that gender is a construct,

and the strength to resist taking your bra off in the middle of the workday.

(It's fine if that last one is not realistically achievable.)

Hold that inhale.

Hold it.

Hold it.

Hold it.

Now, open your mouth and exhale whatever internalized misogyny needs to be released.

Release the idea that you're in competition with other women.

Release the notion that being told you're a "guy's girl" is a compliment.

Release the impulse to make assumptions about other women based on their looks.

Release anything bad you might have said about Britney Spears in the early 2000s.

Release any suggestion, from any source, that trans women are not women. They are.

Release feminism that doesn't take into account the way women's overlapping identities—including race, class, ethnicity, religion, and sexual orientation—impact the way they experience oppression and discrimination.

That's it, let it all out.

Beautiful.

Continue to move from this area of your body, and into other areas that feel tense from exposure to toxic masculinity, tightened by slut-shaming, or stuck—like the many women in the work-force stuck beneath the glass ceiling.

· Apply the same process of breathing in, filling these areas with the female gaze, lesbian TikTok, Lizzo, and that one Fiona Apple album where she's mostly just yelling and banging together a bunch of pots and pans in her living room.

You will begin to notice that the more you focus on your breath, the less you feel compelled to spend every single moment of the day thinking about the wage gap and the infuriating reasons for its continued existence. The more free space that your breath creates, the less space there is to ruminate on the fact that: 1) women make eighty-two cents for every dollar a man makes and 2) the gap is even wider for women of color.

Remember, our breath is the one thing we can always rely on to help us inhale something new—like finally ratifying the Equal Rights Amendment—and exhale something that is no longer serving us—like the entire Republican party.

Once you have finished your mental scan, and you feel less filled with rage, try to reconnect to the rhythm of your breath.

As you inhale once more, say the word "it's" in your mind.

Then, with every exhale, say the word "fine" in your mind.

Inhale "it's."

Exhale "fine."

Inhale "it's."

Exhale "fine."

Continue reciting this mantra until you're no longer overcome with an all-consuming mixture of fury and confusion when I tell you that "At current rates of progress, it will take 257 years to close the economic gender gap."

Keep breathing through those feelings about economic inequality.

If you've lost your mantra, come back to it.

Inhale "it's."

Exhale "fine."

Breathe in through your nose.

Don't think about the fact that women are taxed on menstrual hygiene products.

Breathe out through your mouth.

Breathe in through your nose.

Don't think about the study that showed 95 percent of straight men orgasm every time they have sex, while studies about women's sexual health are still asking if the G-spot exists.

Breathe out through your mouth.

When you're ready to move on, we'll continue.

I'm inviting you now to create even more space—to let go of even more things that no longer serve you.

Let go of apologizing constantly to everyone, even when you've clearly done nothing wrong.

Let go of watching Quentin Tarantino movies because one or more men have insisted you can't know anything about cinema until you do.

Let go of the phrase "I'm not like other girls."

Let go of these things, so you can create space for new things—better things.

Like exploring the possibility that you're bisexual, being grateful that *Roe v. Wade* hasn't been overturned (yet), and having realistic expectations of what a single ten-minute meditation can actually do for your mental health.

You should now be feeling a bit more at ease, a little more free, and able to think of some final things you wish to let go.

Maybe your tendency to start emails with qualifiers like "I just . . ." or "I could be wrong, but . . ."

Maybe you want to let go of those jeans that haven't fit since college but still sit at the bottom of your drawer solely to make you feel bad.

Maybe it's time to let go of dating men who use you as their unpaid therapist because you're preconditioned to perform a disproportionate amount of the emotional labor in relationships.

Think of whatever it is for you, then take a deep breath in and hold that thing with your breath.

Thank that thing for gifting you with numerous exhausting lessons and skill sets that most cis straight men will never have to learn, or even be aware of.

Like how to respond when an unidentified stranger repeatedly gropes your ass during a concert, or how to respond when a man yells, "Looking for some dick?" at you from a moving car, when all you wanted was a bag of Cheez-Its from the bodega.

Feel the gratitude for these beautiful gifts washing over you.

Then, release them.

Now that you have space in your body, in your mind, and in your life, try not to immediately leave and think about how this meditation didn't even address the tip of the bullshit iceberg that women deal with every day just for existing.

Instead, continue to welcome whatever good things have been waiting to land in your life, like another eighteenth-century period drama about women gently brushing hands and staring longingly out at the sea, or another perfume ad featuring Adam Driver as a horse.

Fortify this welcome by putting your hands together over your chest, bowing your head, and setting your intention to make a very large margarita later.

Congratulations on getting through another day as a woman.

Until tomorrow.

Lines from an Honest Gratitude Journal

I AM GRATEFUL THAT EXPRESSING GRATITUDE HAS THE potential to improve my physical and mental health, and that the picture I posted of this gratitude journal is performing so well on social media.

I am grateful that this gratitude journal was in the 70 percent–off bin at Anthropologie.

I am grateful that I also had enough money to buy a full-priced, squirrel-shaped teapot at Anthropologie.

I am grateful for my squirrel-shaped teapot, even though it's not as charming in my kitchen as it was in the Anthropologie display of felt forest animals having an eclectic tea party. Maybe I should've bought the opossum-shaped teapot instead.

I am grateful for opossums. They eat ticks and I'm terrified of Lyme disease.

I am grateful that I have a job that provides health insurance just in case I ever contract Lyme disease.

I am grateful that my job also provides dental insurance, even if it doesn't cover the expensive retainer I had to get because I grind my teeth at night. My gratitude is only marginally lessened by the fact that stress from my job is what made me start grinding my teeth in the first place.

I am grateful for countries that have universal health care. It must be nice.

I am grateful that my workplace has a built-in cafeteria, otherwise I might not be able to work right through my lunch hour.

I am grateful that I have such good work friends. Especially because I've forgotten how to make new friends in any other setting.

I am grateful for the Just Salad franchise near my office. You're not *just* salad to me.

I am grateful to have friends who will immediately tell me when I have spinach stuck in my teeth. I am slightly less grateful for the ones who wait thirty minutes to an hour.

I am grateful that my friends bailed on our plans for this weekend before I could bail on our plans for this weekend.

I am grateful that I have reached an age where most of the men I date have bed frames.

I am grateful that the pullout method is not completely ineffective.

I am grateful that I am no longer dumb enough to fully rely on the pullout method.

I am grateful for lesbians who look like Timothée Chalamet.

I am grateful that my parents still let me use their Netflix account.

I am grateful to the makers of *Bridgerton* for giving me something to watch besides *Outlander*.

I am grateful that there is no longer anyone in my life who makes me watch sports.

I am grateful for all the books on my shelf, and even more grateful that no one knows I've only read 10 percent of them.

I am grateful for the author of the *Ice Planet Barbarians* series, and for all twenty-two of her romance novels about seven-foot-tall, horned blue aliens with insatiable love parasites. I have read 100 percent of them.

I am grateful for true crime podcasts, which confirm all my worst fears about the terrible things that might happen to me every time I leave my house.

I am grateful that I have not yet ended up in a cult, even though I am a perfect candidate.

I am grateful to a sub-brand of American Eagle Outfitters for continuing to make the same style of 100 percent cotton, full-coverage underwear I've been buying since high school.

I am grateful that I no longer feel compelled to pretend that I don't have body hair.

I am grateful that the sun rises each morning, and that I'm not obligated to get up and witness it.

I am grateful for fall, and the bitches who love it.

I am grateful for my bed, and I'd be even more grateful if I never had to get out of it.

I am grateful that my overpriced, squirrel-shaped teapot looks cute sitting on the kitchen counter because, honestly, I never use it.

I am grateful that I won't ever have to figure out what a mortgage is because people in my generation can't afford houses anyway.

I am grateful that this journal is cheaper than therapy.

I am grateful that, aside from the cost of the journal, gratitude is free.

I am grateful to have discovered the miracle of gratitude, which has not yet magically healed my psychic wounds, but probably will any day now.

Have You Tried Taking Care of Something Other Than Yourself?

ON CHICKENS, BABIES, PLANTS, AND SEMI-SENTIENT BLOBS OF SYMBIOTIC BACTERIA.

Have You Tried Backyard Chickens?

THERE ARE OFTEN MOMENTS WHEN ALL MY ATTEMPTS at self-care fall disappointingly flat. I have days where eating a collagen chew, drizzling some hyaluronic acid on my face, or lighting a scented candle just won't cut it. On these days, I wonder if maybe I've got it all wrong. Maybe CBD bath bombs and essential oil diffusers aren't really helping. Maybe they're just more ways to consume convincingly branded health goo. As much as I love trying every kind of health goo—the liquid kind you soak in, the flavored kind you eat in supplement form, the waxy kind you burn—there are times when applying goo to a problem just isn't enough.

On one such occasion, I decided that maybe I needed a deeper kind of self-care, something that involved actual personal growth, like starting therapy or practicing meditation or taking up painting—or maybe some kind of meditative painting therapy. But that all sounded hard and boring. I needed a constructive way to channel all my anxious energy into something productive and fun. Then, it occurred to me that the best way to practice self-care might be to care for something else, something into which I could channel all my anxious energy, but in a way that caused it to thrive. So, I began to consider the following:

Babies

Lots of people seem to be caring for these with varying degrees of satisfaction. After the first year or so, it seems like they offer their caretakers valuable affection and human interaction. Most people describe the experience as rewarding, if not always pleasant. Unfortunately, if you're in possession of a uterus, it looks like people usually expect you to grow your own. That means it's inside of your body for nine months, feeding off you until it claws its way out, after which point you're legally committed to taking care of it for a minimum of eighteen years. Even if I didn't have hypochondriac levels of health anxiety about the whole parasitic gestation process, that's still far too involved for someone who has recently proven that they can't even figure out how to renew their passport properly.

Dogs

These guys provide affection and they're known for being loyal companions. They can be roughly a fifteen-year commitment, depending on the breed and the age at which they're acquired. But unlike babies, there's no chance that they'll go through a phase where their hobbies involve wearing heavy eyeliner, slamming doors, and hating you. They're still a pretty big responsibility though. They need to be walked multiple times a day, and they can't be left alone for too long or there's a chance they'll chew holes in your walls—not ideal if you're renting. Also, most of them require training to prevent them from using your home as an outhouse, doing murders on smaller animals, and running amok in general. That's still a bit more involvement than I'm up for at the moment.

Cats

These are both adorable and more independent than dogs. The fact that they can live for over twenty years doesn't even feel like that big of a commitment because they're so self-sufficient. Therein lies the problem: Because they barely need you, they might spend the duration of their lives hiding under the couch, glaring at you with animal contempt. This would be a chance I was willing to take if it weren't for the litter box. There's just nowhere in my current apartment that I'm willing to store a box of cat poop.

Fish

Watching them swim in sad circles, in their small smelly containers, just makes me even more sad and anxious. I prefer these living free in the wild, or on a plate, battered and fried.

Plants

Just alive enough that it feels bad when you accidentally kill them, but not so alive that their demise rests on your conscience for the rest of your life. They make great decorations, they filter the air—the only drawback is that they don't make great companions. The relationship is a bit one-sided, and I'm looking for something a touch more interactive.

After running through these options and coming up short, I became somewhat disheartened. I did toss around the idea of some edgier, more alternative choices, like getting a rat or becoming a snake person, but those didn't feel right either. Then one afternoon, I came across something I hadn't thought about in years. I was walking by a neighbor's front garden, when one of the rosebushes suddenly began to cluck. I paused and watched as a chicken strutted out from behind the shrubbery. A single beady little dinosaur eye peered up at me from the side of its head. After a moment of piercing, idiotic eye contact, it decided I was not a threat and began to peck at a rock. I heard more soft clucking noises and looked over to see two more hens pecking their way across the garden. I did not move for fear of spooking them, but I was absolutely delighted.

I had been obsessed with the idea of backyard chickens when I was still in school. I'd spent hours procrastinating on assignments by browsing DIY chicken coop instructions and tips for dealing with broody hens. For the longest time, I'd had a copy of *Chickens* magazine displayed prominently on my living room coffee table. When I'd moved to New York after graduation, I'd given up on the idea, but now my backyard chicken fantasies were all coming back. What if taking care of chickens was the thing that would finally make everything okay? I saw the life I wanted flashing before my eyes.

Instead of finding another therapist to help manage my untreated anxiety and depression, I would purchase backyard chickens and everything would be fine. You see, once I got my flock of egg-laying heritage hens, my life would become charmingly simple—just like a farm! Maybe a more rural way of living was the real key to happiness. After all, our ancestors lived simple lives doing backbreaking manual labor on subsistence farms for eighteen hours a day, seven days a week, and they didn't need talk therapy. They also didn't live much past the age of thirty, but who really wants to be thirty-one? Not this psychologically well-adjusted lady.

Sure, some might question the reasoning behind starting a backyard chicken farm as a form of self-care, but we all react to stress differently, right? It's true that some people do need to spend time reflecting on their recent realization that no amount of professional validation will ever be enough to satisfy the yawning pit of inadequacy they've felt growing inside them for as long as they can remember. But other people just need to pour all their energy into owning a beautiful flock of egg-producing birds. Just like some people need cognitive behavioral therapy to manage their anxiety, and some people need a special bond with live poultry. There's really no right way to heal.

Plus, think about how cute a video of chickens frolicking in my backyard would look on Instagram. What would I post if I went to therapy—a video of me sitting on a couch filling out cognitive restructuring worksheets? I think it would be much more therapeutic for me to start a wildly popular Instagram or TikTok account for my chickens. Then, I could use my new platform to spread the word about the many psychological benefits of urban chicken farming, for example:

- Chickens must be bought, and boy do I love buying things— there's nothing quite like amassing possessions to make you feel temporarily whole.

- I'd exclusively keep purebred Rhode Island Whites, Jersey Giants, and rare Russian Orloffs, so the perfectionist high I'd get from their painstaking selection and maintenance would be staggering.

- Reigning over my ideal avian kingdom might even quench my relentless anxiety-fueled need for unwavering control over every aspect of my life—like chicken soup for the obsessive-compulsive soul!

- The increased risk for contracting bird flu and salmonella would be free exposure therapy for my rampant health anxiety.

- Chickens can digest most human food, which means I could put all evidence of emotional eating episodes right into their feed. No sign of eating half a frozen prepackaged cheesecake in the bathtub equals no sign of depression!
- Did I mention that the chickens would provide natural pest control for the garden?

What I think I'd enjoy most, though, is spending time with each of my chickens individually. I'd get to know them and discover all their unique, surprisingly complex personalities—and it would be infinitely more fun than getting to know my own disordered personality. I'd become so knowledgeable that I'd be able to talk about them nonstop in social situations. There'd be no more small talk about the weather or people asking how I'm doing. It'd be all chicken facts, all the time. This would also allow me to avoid any meaningful social interactions that might leave me feeling emotionally vulnerable or exposed. You can't know I'm struggling beneath my hard exterior shell if all I talk about is my newest chicks hatching out of theirs.

After a while, I'd probably be so grateful to the chickens that I'd want to build them a new, larger chicken coop to thank them for their service. I've always felt that nothing says mental and emotional stability like proving to the world that you can build a large, freestanding structure from scratch. If I pulled it off, everyone would have to respect my impressive self-sufficiency. This accomplishment might even make me feel secure enough to stop seeking validation from older male authority figures. There's almost nothing small-scale farming can't fix!

Now, if you're thinking that this whole elaborate fantasy is full of red flags, you wouldn't be wrong. But this is my imaginary backyard farm and I'll pretend raising chickens can fix all of my problems if I want to. It's not my fault that it's easier to find detailed instructions for building a three-story chicken coop than it is to find a reputable therapist who accepts my insurance.

It's so much easier to cross my fingers and hope that chickens or mushroom supplements or a new pair of comfy fuzzy socks is all I need to get my life together. And my desire to take care of something, and to channel my anxious energy into it, is no different.

The thing is, there's nothing wrong with having some adaptive strategies at your disposal for when things get tough. I think most healthy people have at least a few coping mechanisms. If it's not chickens, then it's a weighted blanket, a well-designed meditation app, or a box of Sleepytime tea. They may not solve the root of whatever issue you're having, but they'll tide you over until you can figure things out—the hard and boring part.

However, when a coping mechanism comes in the form of a living, breathing, sentient creature, I'm willing to acknowledge that there's an added level of responsibility involved. Which is why I'm still just fantasizing about my backyard chickens. Because, if I got them now, I'd suck at taking care of us both. It wouldn't be my healing, transcendent, chicken caretaking fantasy, it would be me, a couple of silly birds, and all my anxious energy still exploding in every direction—but with the notable addition of farm fresh eggs. The eggs would be an improvement, sure, but maybe not the one I need right now.

The Pros and Cons of Procreation (As Understood by a Childless Person in Their Twenties)

EVERYONE KNOWS THAT THE BEST WAY TO MAKE A tough decision—like whether or not to create human life with your genitals—is to weigh the pros and cons. So, here are the pros and cons of procreation (as understood by a childless person in their twenties).

Pro: Babies are cute.
Con: Babies are a societally sanctioned form of sleep deprivation torture, and if they weren't so cute, we'd probably consider them a human rights violation.

Pro: Your family's genetic material will carry on into the next generation.
Con: Your family's genetic material will carry on into the next generation.

Pro: You get to see what happens when your genes mix with someone else's.
Con: You get to see what happens when your genetic predispositions toward certain mental health issues mix with someone

else's. What monstrous cocktail of psychological complexes, neuroses, and fixations encased in human flesh might you create?

Pro: You get to experience a unique form of intimacy and emotional connection that no other human bond can replicate.
Con: You get to experience years of being coated from head to toe in another person's bodily fluids. If it comes out of them, it's getting all over you.

Pro: You will have created a new person to hang out with.
Con: You probably won't get to hang out with anyone *but* them until they reach a certain age—roughly the age where they start being fun to hang out with.

Pro: Dinosaur-shaped chicken nuggets are now a totally valid dinner option that you can prepare without shame.
Con: If you ever want to go out for dinner again, it will probably have to be at a place that serves dinosaur-shaped chicken nuggets.

Pro: Your offspring might be some variety of prodigy that makes you very proud to have brought them into the world.
Con: Your offspring might be a bloodthirsty psychopath who collects human eyeballs in glass jars, and you will be the person responsible for unleashing them on the world.

Pro: If you're the one giving birth, you get to experience the miracle of bringing another living human being into existence with your body.
Con: You might also get to experience the miracles of postpartum depression, incontinence, hemorrhoids, hair loss, pelvic

organ prolapse, a torn or surgically sliced perineum, pelvic floor muscle injuries, and/or postnatal PTSD.

Pros: Being a parent makes you a more efficient, more empathetic, and more productive employee overall.
Cons: Being a mother costs women $16,000 in lost wages each year, and research shows employers tend to see mothers as less capable and less committed to their work. The same cannot be said for fathers.

Pro: Being a parent can be tough, but overall, it's a rewarding, unforgettable experience.
Con: If you can afford to reward yourself with a yearly family vacation, it'll either be a trip to Disney World or a camping trip. Both will involve transporting fussy crying children over long distances to see things they probably won't remember in a few years—but it's sure to be an unforgettable experience for you!

Pro: You will have someone who is obligated to take care of you in your old age no matter how troublesome you may become.
Con: You will be obligated to take care of someone for at least eighteen years, but realistically closer to twenty-six years, no matter how troublesome they may become.

Pro: You might start to understand your own parents better.
Con: You might cease to understand the choices of anyone who is not a parent.

Pro: You get to teach a new person about the world.
Con: You get to teach a new person that the world is a systemically unjust place owned by Jeff Bezos, and doomed to become

an endless barren desert surrounded by an acidic boiling ocean.

Pro: You might create the person who finds a solution to climate change and saves us all.
Con: You'll definitely be creating another person whose carbon emissions will contribute to climate change.

Pro: You get to have totally unprotected sex.
Con: It might be the last time you have sex for a very long time.

Pro: You can bring babies to bars now.
Con: Bars are now full of babies.

After collecting the data and weighing the options, the answer to this quandary has become quite clear. Considering all of the preceding pros and cons, the best course of action is to revisit this question again in my thirties. Maybe even my forties. I'm sure I'll know what to do then.

Potential Rebranding Strategies for Cats as a Whole

CATS SUFFER FROM AN IMAGE ISSUE. PEOPLE SAY THEY'RE too independent to be satisfying animal companions, that they're a pet best suited to amusing internet videos and eccentric single women who fill their homes with felines to compensate for their empty wombs. It certainly doesn't help that the press is always pushing narratives like "Dog Saves Child from Burning Building" and "Cats Found to Carry Mind Control Parasites." But when given the opportunity to prove themselves, cats can be wonderful low-maintenance companions. All they need is a little help in the public relations department to get them started. So, whoever is currently managing their image, please consider the following rebranding strategies for cats as a whole:

Current Perception: Cats shed uncontrollably.
Rebrand: Cats lovingly donate their fur to us on a daily basis and it's unfortunate that more people don't appreciate their generosity. Why aren't we making cat hair sweaters? It's an abundant sustainable resource that we just ignore. A conspiracy perpetrated by dog owners and the fashion industry seems likely.

Current Perception: Cats do nothing but sleep.
Rebrand: Cats are masters of self-care, and we should respect them for it. Your cat practices mindfulness by engaging in long bouts of intense staring, prevents burnout by being unconscious for twenty-one out of twenty-four hours a day, and knows how to set clear boundaries by hiding under your bed all day. We could all stand to learn something from their approach to health and wellness.

Current Perception: Cats are assholes.
Rebrand: Cats are mysterious and aloof. Think of them as the animal equivalent of Tilda Swinton: completely unfathomable, bordering on alien, and yet absolutely mesmerizing. They may not listen to you, obey any of your commands, or even acknowledge your existence at times, but that's why it's so special and meaningful when you finally do earn their respect—or at least their desire to scent-mark you as their property.

Current Perception: Cats leave piles of hair vomit all over your house like tiny disrespectful drunk people.
Rebrand: Do you get mad at your dryer for filling up the lint trap? Just like dryers, cats are self-cleaning, and all that vomit is how you know they're still in working order. If your pet isn't leaving puddles of barf all over your bedspread, how can you be sure they're grooming themselves? The Barf Indicator is just one of the many user-friendly features of cat ownership that make them such a great pet.

Current Perception: Multiple cat ownership is for lonely, mentally unstable women.
Rebrand: Multiple cat ownership is the ideal situation for amateur animal behavioral scientists wishing to study intricate social

interactions between members of the feline species. You could be the Jane Goodall of felines, documenting their friendly grooming habits and adorable bonding rituals on social media. Or you might end up being more of a cat prison warden, just doing your best to minimize conflict between violent rival gangs. Either way, there's so much to learn!

Current Perception: *Cats* is Andrew Lloyd Webber's worst musical.
Rebrand: Cats did not actually compel Andrew Lloyd Webber to write this musical, and they're currently pursuing legal damages for injury done to their brand by the latest film adaptation.

Current Perception: Cats poop out mind control parasites.
Rebrand: "Parasite" is a strong word; it implies the host is being detrimentally affected by the presence of the organism. However, after the flu-like symptoms wear off, this bug is hardly even an issue. Don't think of it as a parasite so much as a free bonus pet that comes with every cat. Sure, some scientists say its lasting effects on your brain make you more likely to take risks, but that could be the helpful push you need to finally quit your boring day job and pursue a more rewarding career.

Current Perception: If you die alone in your house, your cat will eat your face (and eventually the rest of you).
Rebrand: This all-too-common anecdote is just a misunderstanding of intent. Cats don't start to callously consume you after you die because they never loved you in the first place. They start to consume you because it's their duty as guardians of the Underworld. In ancient Egypt, they were worshipped as celestial beings, so what better way to be escorted into the afterlife than

through the divine feline digestive tract? Think of them not as opportunistic scavengers, but little furry undertakers.

Current Perception: Cats hunt and torture other animals just for fun.
Rebrand: Okay, so maybe cats are tiny psychopaths, but they're not big enough—or opposable thumbed enough—to turn you into a human lampshade. Since they're limited to prey their own size or smaller, just think of them as the world's most sadistic pest control service.

Current Perception: Cats don't actually like us.
Rebrand: This is patently untrue. As long as you show your cat all the love, affection, and care they deserve as your loyal animal companion, they will absolutely definitely unconditionally tolerate you back.

With these subtle tweaks to the overall Cat brand, their approval rating with the public will surely skyrocket in no time. So, look out, dogs! Cats are making a comeback—after a quick nap. If they feel like it. And it involves food.

Obituaries for All the Plants I've Killed

LET US TAKE A MOMENT TO REMEMBER THE PLANTS
that have given their lives in service of botanical home decor
trends and my repressed desire to nurture something.

Monstera

Monstera deliciosa passed away this morning after a six-month
battle with an unidentified bacterial disease. Monstera was raised
at the Home Depot alongside many other reasonably priced
bacterially infected houseplants. After leaving its disease-ridden
big box nursery, it made its home in a trendy white pot with
questionable drainage. During this time, Monstera sprouted three
new leaves, two of which grew to full size. The third leaf preceded
it into the next life, disintegrating into a soggy brown mess from
suspected overwatering. In the hands of a more skilled caretaker,
Monstera might have recovered from its chronic bacterial illness,
but thanks to botanical incompetence it was taken from us far too
early—at about 5 a.m. with this morning's trash.

Fiddle-Leaf Fig

Today we say farewell to *Ficus lyrata*, known to friends as "Bedroom
Fig Tree." We remember its beauty, charm, and uncanny ability
to make any room look like a picture from a CB2 catalog. In its

youth, it looked so perfect people would often ask if it was real and touch its lush leaves just to be sure. Sadly, its life was cut short by an unfortunate sun exposure accident. After its caretakers left it on an unshaded balcony for roughly two weeks in the heat of a New York City summer, it succumbed to extensive leaf burn. Those closest to Bedroom Fig Tree know it would want to be remembered for how it looked in the prime of its interior design relevance, so the funeral will be a closed-casket affair held in the backyard. Mourners are reminded to wear sunscreen.

Elephant Bush

It is with a heavy heart that we say goodbye to *Portulacaria afra*. This beloved Elephant Bush came into the life of its caretaker as a surprise housewarming gift from a friend and has left this world just as suddenly. Despite meticulous efforts not to overwater the sun-loving succulent, its caretaker woke up one morning to find that it had died in the night, much like the friendship it once represented. The hole its passing has left will not be easy to fill, mostly because it was the only plant that fit nicely into the frustratingly odd dimensions of the small windowsill it occupied.

Satin Pothos

Today we honor the life of *Scindapsus pictus*, a plant known for its bravery, tenacity, and ability to live in a dimly lit bathroom. Its caretaker fondly remembers how Bathroom Pothos persevered in its harsh environment, wrapping its long tendrils around the bathroom mirror just like they once saw in a product shot from UrbanOutfitters.com. This gave them immeasurable joy and satisfaction, and they never once guessed that the location would lead to Bathroom Pothos's ultimate doom come winter. It was far too late by the time anyone noticed how close its vines were to the unforgiving chill of the bathroom window. Now, the only thing colder than its shriveled leaves is the grief-stricken heart of its bereft caretaker, who really thought they were doing a pretty good job this time, honestly. Bathroom Pothos is survived by a small cutting taken during the summer. The cutting is expected to be potted in the spring, providing it survives past infancy in its current container, a beer stein full of water next to the kitchen sink. Bathroom Pothos will surely be watching over it from the great garden in the sky.

Umbrella Tree

Schefflera actinophylla passed away this week at two years old. Its hobbies included helpful air purification and being in the way of the closet door. It won its first battle with scale insects last year after several treatments, which required its caretaker to drench it in soapy water and scrape the foul little pests off by hand. It looked like it was in full remission this year, until the revolting bugs made a startling comeback. As one of the longest surviving plants in the house, its passing is truly devastating to those who cared for it—excluding, of course, the household cat, who resented not being allowed to chew its poisonous leaves like a furry little idiot.

String of Pearls Plant

This week we lay to rest *Senecio rowleyanus*, affectionately known as "Pearl," a beautiful succulent and recent addition to the living room bookcase. Tragically, Pearl's pot was recently discovered to be brimming with baby centipedes—absolutely bursting with millions of repulsive little legs and shiny writhing bodies. It had been brought home from the hip new plant store/coffee shop around the corner only days before. Due to dire, icky, bug-related circumstances, the family opted for immediate and thorough cremation over a traditional burial, just to be safe. A lawsuit against the plant store/coffee shop for emotional damages is expected to follow.

Lipstick Plant

We will never forget *Aeschynanthus radicans* or its red tube-like flowers that were kind of a bitch to clean up every time they bloomed and fell all over the floor. It was four years old when it died this past weekend in a terrible airplane accident. The accident was, of course, thinking it was okay to take a houseplant on an airplane. The stress of having all its glorious vines smushed into a duffel bag for the duration of a cross-country flight was, unsurprisingly, too much for it. In lieu of flowers, which have become emotionally triggering for its guilt-ridden caretaker, mourners have been asked to make a donation to Learning a New Leaf, an organization dedicated to teaching former plant murderers basic plant care techniques.

Cactus in a Teacup with Two Other Succulents

Gymnocalycium mihanovichii, a.k.a. Lil' Spiky Guy, died suddenly this week at the age of seven and a half months. It came from a Saturday farmers market in Washington Square but resided in Brooklyn for the majority of its short life. It shared an eclectic floral teacup with two other adorable miniature succulents, looking just like the Pinterest post that inspired their purchase. Its caretaker was in shock when Lil' Spiky Guy's condition rapidly deteriorated, going from proudly phallic to soggy and deflated in a matter of hours. It was eventually found to have died due to complications resulting from overwatering. It is survived by its teacup mates, Hen and Chicks and Baby Jade, who are understandably traumatized, but glad to have a little more space in their adorable death trap of a container.

Hen and Chicks and Baby Jade

We must regretfully announce the passing of both *Sempervivum "Hen and Chicks" globiferum* and *Crassula "Baby Jade" ovata*. They were attached at the root in this life and so shall they be in the next. They are preceded by their comrade Lil' Spiky Guy and go to join him now in that great big teacup in the sky. They leave behind a grieving caretaker, who really has no idea what they did wrong—they used the special succulent soil and drainage rocks and everything. Suspected cause of death is someone looking at them too aggressively.

Air Plant

Tillandsia ionantha, who went by "Air Plant," was laid to rest today at the age of three months, two weeks, and four days. Air Plant enjoyed air, looking cool, and hanging in its elaborate brass plant cage. Because of its carefree Zen aesthetic, it was easy to underestimate the level of care Air Plant required. Despite a meticulous soaking and drying schedule involving multiple phone alarms and calendar reminders, tragedy struck this winter. Unfortunately, Air Plant's cause of death is still unknown and internet searches have yielded few results. Perhaps it was too much air? Not enough air? A sudden loss of will to live? Its defeated caretaker is left with only two options in the wake of its passing: 1) accepting that everything they try to nurture is doomed to wilt and die or 2) accepting that it is time to buy fake plants.

What to Expect When You're Expecting Kombucha

FIRST OFF, CONGRATULATIONS! YOU'RE NOW THE PROUD parent of a mother—or SCOBY, if you prefer the technical term—and in just a few days your sweet bundle of Symbiotic Cultures of Bacteria and Yeast will be giving birth to a delicious, fermented tea beverage. This can be both an exciting and fraught experience, especially if it's your first time taking responsibility for a cloudy, rubbery mass of hungry microorganisms. That's why we, the kombucha experts, have put together this helpful guide—so you know exactly what to expect when you're expecting kombucha.

Prepping Before You're Expecting

Before you bring your precious SCOBY home, there are some preparations that need to be made for its arrival. You'll need a gallon-sized pot, a funnel, some cheesecloth, black or green tea, sugar, and a large rubber band for feeding your SCOBY. You'll also need a large glass jar for containing it. We recommend one with steep edges in case it develops centralized intelligence and tries to crawl out. If you have pets, now is a good time to sit them down and let them know you'll be adding a new member to the family. Make sure to explain that just because you'll be taking care of millions of bacteria now doesn't mean you love them any less. You can also start familiarizing them with the smell of vinegar and the sound of microscopic shrieks of hunger, which only animals can hear. That way they won't be alarmed when both things fill your home.

Meeting Your Mother

Once your home is prepared for a SCOBY, you can set about acquiring one. We know some people choose to grow their own SCOBY from store-bought kombucha, but we don't feel comfortable supporting large SCOBY breeders when there are so many mothers out there in need of adoption. Not to mention, you could end up supporting an inhumane kombucha mill—a place that uses artificial flavors and clear glass bottles. They're practically a death sentence for most probiotics. Kombucha is just a profitable beverage to them, not a beautiful, lovable liquid made of living beings. For that reason, we recommend finding someone who already has a mother and is willing to rip off a piece for you to adopt.

Let's Get Brewing

It's time to put your new SCOBY in the large jar you prepared for it and brew its first batch of tea. This can be an important bonding moment for you and your sweet little bundle of microbes. The tea you brew for your SCOBY now, when it's just starting to produce kombucha, can have profound effects for the rest of its life. It might be hard to believe, but the quality of the tea you choose could be the difference between your kombucha being bush league or Ivy League. You're probably thinking, "My kombucha hasn't even been born yet and you already want me to start putting pressure on it to excel? Surely that kind of thing can wait until it's older." Wrong! Don't make this kombucha parenting mistake. If you want your kombucha to be the best it can be, you need to start meticulously cultivating it from the first seconds of its gestation. Your SCOBY *lives* in that tea. It *eats* that sugar. If you use anything but the finest organic loose-leaf black or green tea and 100 percent organic cane sugar to brew its food, it'll be doomed to a life of mediocrity and failure. We also recommend putting a pair of headphones on the container and playing some Mozart while it feeds. You want it to develop good taste early, and you'll be glad you did when your kombucha emerges more cultured than all the rest.

What You May Be Wondering about Fermentation

Now that you've fed your mother SCOBY, you get to witness the beautiful natural process of fermentation. Store the container in a safe, dark place, which will act as a sort of incubator, and check on it every couple days. Contrary to popular belief, the way the mother floats in the tea is not an indication of whether the resulting kombucha will be male or female. In fact, we ask that you refrain from imposing gender on your probiotic drinks— most bacteria are fiercely sexually fluid. These five to seven days of intense fermentation will be full of anticipation, but try to resist the urge to check on your kombucha too often. You don't want to encourage needy or codependent behavior from your bacteria at such a crucial stage. Instead, spend this time preparing the various social media posts you'll be launching to make sure that everyone knows you make your own kombucha now. If your friends are going to insist on clogging your feed with their dumb babies, you're going to clog theirs with your beloved bacterial spawn. Perhaps try a caption like, "Say hello to kombucha batch #1! It's thirty-two fluid ounces and its mother is doing great!" or "Isn't it beautiful? You can see so much of its mother floating around in it already."

Flavoring and Beyond

The day you harvest your first fully fermented batch of kombucha is one you'll never forget. It might take a few days to get exactly the right balance of sweet and sour, but you'll intuitively know when it's ready to come out and meet the world. Once you've gotten over the initial awe of holding that first little miracle bottle in your arms, there are a few things you'll need to consider, like whether to leave your kombucha unflavored. This particular choice usually comes down to your personal or religious beliefs. If you decide to go for a flavor, you'll need to add the fruit of your choice, seal it in an airtight container, and shove it back into its dark womb-like cabinet to ferment for another one to three days. This can be somewhat traumatizing for the kombucha because this process also carbonates it—which has occasionally been known to end in tragic container explosions. You can't treat your kombucha like it's made of glass forever though! Even if the container is actually made of glass and that's why it explodes under pressure.

Ultimately, it's your kombucha and your responsibility to make decisions in its best interest. At least until the day it mutates its fractured horde of bacterial life-forms into one united, sentient organism capable of rational thought. For your own safety, we highly recommend drinking it before that day.

An Inconclusive Conclusion

I HAVE TRIED A LOT OF THINGS IN THE NAME OF FEEL-ing better. I've been hypnotized and herbally cleansed. I've been cupped and crystaled and abdominally massaged. I've bought overpriced uncomfortable underwear sets, posture-correcting tech devices, and trendy Instagram dresses that would look more at home in an adaptation of *Little Women* than in my life. I've attempted to lift, tone, and burn myself into an unattainable shape. I've tried making my life all about my job, and I've tried disappearing completely into books. I've gulped down water like a fish and eaten like a carb-hating dinosaur for months. Some of these things kind of worked, and some of them absolutely did not. Most of them were impulsive, isolated shots in the dark—the "I'll try anything" approach to feeling better.

Lately, I've started to feel like the call for people to practice self-care is just another version of telling people to pull themselves up by their bootstraps. Don't worry about the shortcomings of our deeply flawed healthcare system; you can just take this magic herbal supplement. Don't challenge patriarchal ideas about beauty; they won't affect you if you do this antiaging cleanse. Don't expect your employer to respect boundaries and provide work-life bal-ance; it's up to you to exercise all your chronic stress and tension away. These small acts of self-care might make you feel better temporarily, but they're probably not fully addressing larger issues that you can't solve alone.

I think going forward, the answer to feeling better might not be in self-care, but in taking better care of each other. At the risk of sounding sappy, the things that have helped me the most out of all my many attempts are the things that have involved some element of human connection. Going running makes me feel good, but it feels better when I go with my best friend. I didn't get a Peloton because I love biking, I got it because it comes with a weird culty exercise community. Eating some diet-approved dinner never feels as good as eating literally anything with people I love. Being hypnotized was cool, but it was only a meaningful experience because the hypnotist—bless his heart—took the time to connect with me and help me work through all my inexplicable crying. Even when I withdraw into my romance novels, I'm still reading stories that are centered around people's relationships with each other—or, you know, their relationships with big blue aliens. I think I've probably been quietly aware of this for a while because, otherwise, I would've already moved to the woods to live in my nightmare shack.

It's fine if you still like to wind down by lighting candles, drinking green juice, or doing some spiritual leader's patented deep-breathing exercises. Most self-care stuff is relatively harmless. But I don't think it hurts to remember that we probably also need other people—a support network of friends, family, partners, workplaces, and communities—if we're going to feel better in a real, sustainable way. As much as I don't want it to be true, you just can't replace people with adaptogen dust and aromatherapy. Believe me, I've tried. For better or worse, I think we are each other's best caretakers, and we can do a better job of it than any brand selling a magical self-care solution.

That said, I'm still far from having things all figured out. So when it comes to happiness and the unending task of existing in general, I intend to just keep trying.

Acknowledgments

I WOULD FIRST LIKE TO THANK MY FAMILY AND FRIENDS for their love and support. According to several internet personality tests of varying legitimacy, I am a delicate flower that requires an above-average amount of both, and you've never let me wilt.

Brittain McNeel, you were the first person I ever shared my writing with, and since you did not tell me to stop immediately and take up knitting instead, one might argue that the existence of this book is almost entirely your fault. For that I will be forever grateful. I cannot thank you enough for reading early drafts, talking me through my many meltdowns, and just believing I could do this in general. There's no one I'd rather eat Jell-O with every day because life is a fucking nightmare.

Ross Wolinsky, thank you for reading a draft of almost every single essay in this book, even when you would rather have been making art with your beep-boop-bop wires and boxes. I'm lucky to have you and your very smart funny brain in my life.

Special thanks to my brother David, who keeps me humble by reminding me who the real artist is in the family; Tara Lawall, who has always given me good writing advice, even when she claims not to know what she's doing; Chen Liang, who made me a second Cup of Shame so that I would have a set; Allie Carr, who made me a friendship bracelet to remind me that she thinks I'm a genius (not true, but I'm still grateful); and Teddy Malenfant, Katie Schaller, Matthew Carroll, Jason Goldberg, Aja Gabel, Jesse Donaldson, Cathy Burrows, Nigel Burrows, Emily Hovis, Anne Marie Wonder, Aunt Moe, Uncle Doug, my wonderful parents, and anyone else who ever said a kind word to me while I was writing.

Some of the essays in this book originally appeared on *McSweeney's Internet Tendency*; many thanks are owed to editor Chris Monks for giving me a chance and running my work before anyone else. Your rejection letters are kinder than most people's acceptance letters.

Thanks are also due to everyone at Chronicle Prism, especially my editor Cara Bedick, who plucked me out of the vast ocean of the internet and guided me gently through this whole process; the wonderful designers, who good-humoredly entertained my requests for a slightly more dead-eyed smiley face on the front cover; and the copy editors who tried their very best to make me sound smarter than I actually am.

Endless thanks as well to my literary agent Allison Devereux at The Cheney Agency for answering every one of my dumb questions and panicked emails with the patience of a saint. I've been so happy to have you on my team.

To my creative directors at Wieden + Kennedy, Darcie Burrell, Azsa West, Devin Gillespie, and Becca Wadlinger, thank you for letting me leave work for three months to do something that was not advertising. It was so much easier to write knowing that I had both your collective blessing and uninterrupted health-care coverage.

Finally, thanks to Rob. If it weren't for you, I might still be lying under my kitchen table crying, and I'd definitely still be organizing my writing in a way that resembles the *It's Always*

Sunny in Philadelphia conspiracy board meme. You were an impenetrable six-foot wall of love, emotional stability, and comfort throughout this whole messy thing. For that, you have my unending gratitude and all my love.

About the Author

MADELEINE TREBENSKI HAS WRITTEN FOR *MCSWEENEY'S Internet Tendency*, the *New Yorker*, and *Outside* magazine. Her work is included in the collection *Embrace the Merciless Joy: The McSweeney's Internet Tendency Guide to Rearing Small, Medium, and Large Children* and has appeared on Elizabeth Banks's *My Body, My Podcast*.